Changing the World Within

The Dynamics of
Personal and Spiritual Growth

Joseph A. Grassi

PAULIST PRESS
New York/Mahwah

Copyright ©1986
by Joseph A. Grassi

Library of Congress
Catalog Card Number: 85-62871

ISBN: 0-8091-2755-5

Published by Paulist Press
997 Macarthur Boulevard
Mahwah, New Jersey 07430

Printed and bound in the United States of America

Contents

To Carolyn my wife
whose love and inspiration
have made this book possible

Introduction

This book is drawn from the experience of a class each year in Personal and Spiritual Growth given at the University of Santa Clara. I have been very gratified by the enthusiastic response of so many students young and old. Much of what is presented here is the product of insights that came through working with them. Their reactions have prompted me to write up the basic elements of our process in a form suitable for individuals as well as for classes and groups.

The last decade has witnessed an amazing growth of weekends, seminars, workshops, books, etc., dedicated to furthering the process of personal growth. However, in most of these the spiritual dimension is almost entirely lacking. I have become convinced that this means a serious repression of the basic Source of energy needed to bring about effective change. On the other hand, a purely spiritual approach runs the risk of giving insufficient attention to the dynamics of everyday relationships and events that are the human context of personal growth. This book presents an integrated, holistic approach. This includes Spirit, soul, mind, emotions and body.

The approach in this book is ecumenical in the sense of not being attached to any particular religious affiliation. At the same time, it has a broad Christian and biblical base, though not in an exclusivist sense. Many insights have been drawn from Eastern religions as well as from the modern human potential movement. While this book contains many helpful techniques and practical exercises, it emphasizes that life itself, in all its fullness, is our best teacher once we become aware of its amazing opportunities and unlimited energies. With this in mind, the book intends to be a practical guide in the all important matter of personal and spiritual growth. The format of the book is arranged so that it can be used by groups, classes or individuals.

1

The Giant First Step: Taking Responsibility for Life

Each one of us would like to feel that our personal journey through life on spaceship earth will somehow be a contributing factor toward creating a better world. Yet discouragement often sets in after a realistic glance at the world around us where violence, crime, war and insensitivity surround us on every side. It often seems a hopeless task to accomplish even a small amount of significant change. The modern individual feels very much alone and helpless. The temptation is either to ''drop out'' or simply drift through life doing a bit of good here and there and grasping at whatever happiness comes our way.

The surprising truth, however, is that we have never had so great an opportunity for effective change both in ourselves and in the world we live in. The necessary climate for such change is a time of urgent crisis, and this we indeed have! The second step is a deep awareness of this crisis. This can unleash all the unlimited possibilities and potential for rapid personal and spiritual growth that could soon transform both ourselves and the world we live in. This chapter is meant to outline the first giant step toward such an awareness.

Let us start with two examples, one from nature and one from personal relations. Then we will formulate the lessons derived from each. First of all, take a sunrise, or sunset. What keeps us from experiencing a deep communion or sense of oneness with these marvelous events of nature which are for human beings the most important events in the universe each day? Oneness and communion mean that separating space disappears or is greatly reduced. What is this separating space?

Let us imagine that we suddenly have an enthusiastic impulse to go out and watch that beautiful sunset. What happens when we do this? Actually, the first time we ever really experienced a sunset, we were deeply moved and absorbed. We were little children completely enthralled in one of the greatest happenings on earth. Now that we are older, what happens? We fasten our eyes on the fiery orb moving toward the horizon. But almost immediately, a flood of thoughts and words come into the mind such as: "What a beautiful sunset," or "This is like another sunset on another occasion," or "This is better or not as beautiful as another," or we think of ways we could describe the sunset.

What is happening? The experience of oneness, a really silent communion, has been choked by a flood of thoughts, the product of a rational mind. This leads on to comparisons, contrasts, verbalizations, descriptions that could go on endlessly.

A second example is that between two friends, two lovers or two spouses. We all vividly recall deep encounters when we knew we really loved each other. It was something beyond words or thoughts. Silent, deep communion was characteristic of these times. There was also a total attention to one another: eyes, ears, touch, mind, feelings all came together and were focused on that person.

As time went on, however, I began to think a lot about the relationship. I built up a file or catalogue of thoughts and memories about this person. These were comparisons, contrasts, judgments about him or her. For example, is this person of the "right" age or appearance? Are this person's politics, religion, preferences, joys and pleasures the same as my own? Little by little I built up an internal image about this person based on past experiences with that person and with many other people. As a result, more and more, when I see that person, I see him or her in terms of an *image in my mind* that has gradually been built up. As a consequence, I see such persons *not as they are* but as I have made them, or want them to be.

Now let us analyze the above two examples. What has brought about a barrier of separation between myself and the sunset, or another person? It is the fact that I have become an observer or analyzer through a chain of thought. This has created a space of separation. Oneness or communion is caused by breaking down separating space. This breakdown is accomplished by *relationships*. The word "relationship" comes from *re-latio*, from the Latin, *latus* or side. Things or people who touch side by side and affect each other are in relationship.

In contrast, when thoughts become the vehicle of dealing with others, another process takes place. I see people and the world not as they are in themselves, but in terms of the thoughts, images, models and expectations I have built up in my mind. This creates distance and space between us. It also results in a very conditional type of love. When people conform to my images and expectations, I love them. When they do not, I have little use for them. It means also that I do not live in the *real present,* for my encounters with others become based on thoughts, and memories which belong to the past.

Now let us look at some of the consequences of a thought- or image-centered approach. As we have seen above, we tend to live in the past and become locked in past memories and experiences. Or on the other hand, our mind goes to the future, hoping that new persons or situations will fit our models and expectations. The present moment becomes very ordinary, or even boring. Our freedom also becomes lost. We become prisoners of thought patterns. "Shoulds" and "shouldn'ts" dominate our actions instead of a beautiful free-flowing sensitivity to others through relationships.

Our lives also become dominated by fear, especially of death. Our thought system and memories become the only pattern we know. If we lost that, what do we have? We hang on to what we feel we really have and know, which becomes the great certainty of our lives. We become afraid to go out into the new and unknown which might be a new person we meet, an unexpected event, sickness or even death. Life becomes dominated by thought, not relationships.

Another consequence is an exaggerated dependence on others instead of the beautiful, free interdependency that comes through relationship with others as equals. Depending on thought and reason, we look to others' leadership for advice, or we search for authority figures whom we can follow. This leads to an excessive desire to please others and win their favor by accepting their opinions or values (mind dependence). It also leads to dependence on outside ideologies (thought systems) as "saviors." This might be, for example, capitalism or communism. Or it could be a particular set of beliefs in the form of an organized religion. (I am not speaking of that type of religion based on an inner movement toward or relationship to God.) It could be a passive, unconditioned loyalty to some group, community or government.

Another result is a life burdened by constant competition with others. Our minds are constantly judging and making comparisons as well as contrasts. We try harder and harder to succeed because we judge our actions in terms of others' actions as well as expectations. We become obsessed with "doing things," because our thoughts must be placed in action. We become "product-oriented" not only in the sense of making products, but in terms of buying them.

This leads to a particular view of time. Time is valuable to the extent that we can get things done, or get other people to act or conform to our thoughts and models. Time is being continually watched and measured. We are afraid to lose time. In contrast, every relationship is essentially timeless for it depends on a *state of being,* not some measured action. In a deep relationship, with total attention, time disappears and gives way to eternity.

Most dangerous of all, the thought-centered person is driven to *control* both the events and persons of his or her life. Thus such persons become, even unconsciously, very power-centered. When people do not agree or go along with their thoughts or models, they have little use for them or avoid them. In extreme cases (but all too frequent) non-conformists are punished or even eliminated. As my thought and model system expands and broadens, I become more and more defensive since I have much more to protect and guard. My own "department of defense" is continually building up its arsenal of "weapons" to protect the increased territory and borders.

Moving from individuals to groups and nations we see that the latter are really only expansions of the individual dilemma. Just as individuals, nations continually increase their departments of defense to defend artificially expanded economic borders. War and economic power become accepted means of dealing with nations that are a threat to what we feel we should have. When some of the world's great religions become exclusive sets of beliefs, rather than an inner spirit, we have seen what horrors can result: "heretics" or non-conformers can be severely punished or even put to death. The Middle Ages' Crusade to "liberate" the Holy Land became a great blood-letting and looting operation that shocked the world. Moslem armies in the past have made converts at the point of the sword.

Communism as an exclusive ideology has been spread through the world mainly by violence and murder. Capitalism has done little better both by war and by making most of the third world economic slaves. Rabid followers of particular parties have sometimes put aside ethical considerations and resorted to all kinds of unfair tactics merely to get their candidates elected.

Is there any remedy or solution for the prison of violence and power that this world becomes as the result of our thought-dominated human beings? There are many attempted solutions. For example: People have made use of drugs and alcohol, which have become a world industry almost second to armaments. This however is a temporary escape which dulls or quiets the mind only for a time and also damages, sometimes irreparably, our bodies. It is also a use of an outside force which can create dependency or other dangerous consequences. We cannot conquer thought by attempting to suppress or eliminate it.

It has been said that people need motivation: rewards and punishments have been used for thousands of years by parents, by religion, by communities and nations. However, rewards and punishments produce only short-time results. They tend to make us act for ulterior motives—money, pleasure, prestige or avoidance of pain or loss—and produce no radical change. In fact, in the long run they make us more slaves of our thought systems by reinforcing them. Only the action done in total attention, in deep relationship, for its own sake is a completely personal act.

So we ask again, "How can we get at the roots of the violence, crime and war on our spaceship earth?" Even this question is deceptive, for it leads us outside of ourselves to some reason, principle or thought that can be analyzed. The actual answer or solution is only found in the question and the questioner: *I am the world.* The horrible violence in the world is within myself. As a result, *I take responsibility* and place it separately on no one else. I am a prisoner of a thought-centered mind—just like everyone else. My first step is to be completely and emotionally aware of this and accept it. *This is who I am.* I take responsibility too for what happens in the world, for I am its cause. The process of changing the world can only begin with myself. As it does, it will move in concentric contagious waves to others as well—but that is not my motivation, but a consequence of taking responsibility.

The above first step, if total and complete, is enough to start a radical change in myself/the world. Responsibility is the same as relationship. *Respondo* (Latin, I reply) because I am *re-latus* (at the side of, or one with other). When this begins to happen, I experience a beautiful new inner freedom, not dependent on separating thoughts. Once I deeply respond and relate, my whole life-style takes a new form that can only be described by the term "passionate living." It means living with total attention and sensitivity to every person and creature in the universe. It means a deep listening—not only with ears, but with eyes, hands and whole being to others and acting accordingly. *It does not mean that thoughts and memories disappear; it means that they make their own partial but valuable contribution* to total attention and commitment.

Now for some of the characteristics of this new inner freedom. It is a commitment not to a system, a set of values, or a thought but to the entire structure of life. It is total, full of feeling, active and instantaneous for it responds to people and situations as they are by touching them through relationship. It is independent, a "do-it-yourself" way. It works with others, often in silent communion, as companions, equals and inter-dependents. It is effortless and free, for it flows from deep within and does not depend on exterior motivation. In daily life, such an inner freedom results in a beautiful freshness and newness. A sunrise or sunset is experienced with all the wonder of a child. Old friends are like good, old wine. New friends are like sparkling, new champagne.

The problems in the world around us are experienced in a new way: I see the problem first in myself and tend to identify. Also, more and more I see all problems as inter-related; for example, if I am jealous or angry and feel it, everything I do is jealousy or anger. I see this in myself and the world around me. I find a new confidence in life itself and in relationships; I have less confidence in so-called "solutions," based on thought systems alone. In this respect, I become more and more a doubter and questioner while growing in confidence.

Thoughts and memories will still be an important part of my life. The difference will be in my awareness of them. As this grows, the time-less, silent and deep period in between thoughts will also have a much more important and frequent part to play in my life.

In the remainder of our book we will try to spell this all out much more in detail so that the commitment to personal and spiritual growth may quickly and deeply take root in our lives.

Points for group or class discussion as well as individual reflection:

1. Why is it easier for a child than an adult to become totally involved in a beautiful experience? How can I recover this ability?

2. What are the causes of "conditional love" for others? Think of several examples.

3. How do we set up (perhaps unwittingly) individual "departments of defense"? What insights does this provide about the solution of larger society as well as international conflicts?

4. Why are rewards and punishments insufficient to produce radical change? Think of some examples from your own personal experience.

5. What is the first step I must take to get at the roots of violence, crime and evil in the world? Draw up several concrete resolutions for putting this into effect.

Annotated Bibliography for Further Reading

Keyes, Ken, Jr., *The Hundredth Monkey* (Coos Bay, Oregon: Vision, 1982). The author is convinced that we have the creativity and power to change ourselves and our world by taking an important first step in regard to the uses of nuclear energy.

Krishnamurti, J., *You Are the World* (N.Y.: Harper, 1972). One of the great philosophers of our time points out how the awakening of real intelligence begins when we take responsibility for the world we live in and identify with it.

Mische, Gerald and Patricia, *Toward a Human World Order* (Ramsey, N.Y.: Paulist, 1977). These two founders of Global Education Associates describe concrete strategies for leaders and ordinary people to use in order to bring about peace and global unity.

2

Meditation—
The Listening Heart

God may be described as the supreme Listener of the universe. When he revealed himself to Moses in a burning bush at Sinai he said,

> I have seen the affliction of my people who are in Egypt and have heard their cry because of their taskmasters; I know their sufferings, and I have come down to deliver them out of the hand of the Egyptians (Ex 3:7–9).

This revelation of Moses is central to the three great western world religions, Christianity, Judaism and Moslemism, because it marks the beginnings of God's intervention in history to save his people. At the very essence of it all is a God who listens, sees and knows his people, for he is their Creator and Protector.

Consequently, the highest quality to which a human being can aspire is that of being a total listener, like the God who fashioned him or her. In Hebrew, this quality is called "a listening heart." This is beautifully described in the Bible through the stories of King Solomon who is presented during his youth as a patron and model of wisdom (1 Kgs 3—5). One feast day, Solomon offered a thousand holocausts, symbolic of his desire to give himself entirely to God. That night he had a dream in which he heard God say to him, "Ask whatever you wish and I will give it to you (1 Kgs 3:5). Solomon replied, "Give your servant an understanding heart to govern your people and to discern between good and evil; for who is able to govern this great people of yours?"

The "understanding heart" in this text is literally in Hebrew a "listening heart." It is a quality that can make him like God in his supreme quality of listener to his people. It is so much God's own characteristic that it is a special gift, given in answer to prayer. The biblical text notes that God bestowed this gift on Solomon: "I now do according to your word. I give you a heart so wise and understanding that there has never been anyone like you before your time" (3:12). The gift of a "listening heart" enables Solomon not only to listen to his people and make wise decisions; it also makes him a keen observer and listener to all the universe around him: "He discussed trees, from the cedar of Lebanon to the hyssop that grows out of the wall; he spoke also of beasts, of birds, of reptiles, and of fish" (4:33).

However, it is not really possible to listen to other people and the universe around us unless we first learn to listen to ourselves. This is true of God also, who first of all knows himself, and hence is able to know the whole universe. This is why we pointed out in Chapter 1 that the first step to growth is full and total awareness of who we really are. It is here that meditation plays an essential role—but not meditation as a "practice," but meditation that goes on during every moment of life. To most people the very word "meditation" conveys the image of something esoteric and mysterious—perhaps someone sitting in one of those impossible crosslegged positions, motionless as a statue with incense burning and perhaps a statue of Buddha nearby. In fact, some meditation systems do actually claim to have special secrets they can teach us, usually only through special teachers and a schedule of fees—often high. It is easy to get the idea that meditation is a practice open only to a relatively few, and then only after long practice, severe asceticism, and continual discipline.

However, the true meaning of meditation is found in the very root of the word itself. This is from the Latin root *medi,* "in the middle of," and *"stare,"* "to stay in." It means nothing more than to go to the center of our being, or "center" ourselves. It means to be *who we really are* in the depth of our being. This is something that is open to all of us. It is part of life itself. Sometimes we do it spontaneously or informally, sometimes by definite formal efforts. It is being truly aware of who we are at every level of our being. Another way to express this is the following: To meditate means to be fully conscious of ourselves, the people around us, of nature, and the world we live in. As we do so we will gradually arrive to the ultimate reality and oneness of the universe we live in.

Another obstacle is the drive that we all have to "accomplish something,'' or to see some fruit, or definite result of our actions. For example, often when I do some writing, my mind goes to that nice, finished, beautifully bound copy on the bookstands; I imagine the newspaper and magazine reviews; I anticipate and hope for a favorable popular reception, and, yes, even some fat royalty checks. My children, now teenagers, frequently interrupt, and my wife stops me to ask about various matters. All this is part of the life-process of writing a book. This is where I am. The process is more important than the product. The process is personal and full of life; the product is only an object. Writing a book can be truly meditative when I concentrate on the process more than the product. This is hard with the pressures of the culture we live in. The fruits of action are sought much more than the action itself. We look beyond our actions and work for the rewards, the fruits, the pay-off. Or we look for the ''grades'' in school rather than the joy and discovery of learning. In writing my book, the ''interruptions'' are greater opportunities for growth than the undisturbed moments of silence (even though they may delay the nice finished product).

Another fear we have is that of ''doing nothing.'' Is this not idleness? It is interesting that according to most state and local laws, it is actually forbidden to stand on a street corner doing nothing. We could be arrested for ''loitering.'' In fact, I see many signs on properties nearby in the Santa Cruz mountains here in California that say, ''No Trespassing or Loitering.'' We are a very action-oriented society, and western technological progress has accentuated this. This does not mean that when we meditate we stop acting, as we have already seen. However, it does mean that there will be some times when we will cease outward actions, and be content to be quietly aware of our being itself, rather than any action. At times it is necessary to slow down the relentless fast moving lives we lead, come to a full stop, and find out who we are and where we are going.

But is not social action, care and service of others the highest form of life? Yes it is, but there is no conflict between this and meditation. The source of loving service for others is a heart that is aware, sensitive and conscious of one's own feelings and the feelings of others—the very goal of meditation. This can never fail to produce true social action. However, without this, it could be task-oriented or a power trip for ourselves that treats others as objects to fulfill a mental ideal or duty.

But is not meditation somehow an escape from reality? On the contrary, meditation engages in reality and moves to its depth. Recently, I was driving along the highway and saw an advertisement that struck my eye. It read, "Not by bread alone does man exist but by Straw Hat Pizza." I was at first amused by this, and then somewhat offended because it was taken from a biblical statement, "Not by bread alone does man exist but by every word that comes from the mouth of God (Dt 8:3, quoted by Jesus in Mt 4:4). The biblical meaning of the text is that there is a deeper meaning in bread as we eat and experience God himself as the source of life, earth, bread, and all nourishment. In fact, when Jesus broke bread with others, he did so with such reverence, and obvious consciousness of its meaning that it was especially noticed by others. Luke tells us that the two disciples on the way to Emmaus on Easter Sunday recognized Jesus as he began to break bread with them (24:35). Meditation does not consist in getting away from people or things or nature but by communicating with them at deeper levels.

Are there not quicker ways of raising our consciousness and awareness than meditation? It has been said that some drugs can accomplish in a few moments what years of meditation could not obtain. It is true that drugs have been helpful to some people when administered with great care and with professional help and guidance. But there are two main dangers, to put it very simply: death and insanity. To illustrate, we have many levels of consciousness—every person is like a many-storied skyscraper. We can move to various floors of this skyscraper gradually, through meditation, and then return to our ordinary levels of consciousness. But if we try to do so by violent means, our elevator can get stuck on one story or level and be unable to return—which means insanity. Or our elevator can lose control of itself through violent, unrestrained action—which could result in serious injury or death. Meditation is gentle and flowing, the very opposite of violent and controlling. Drugs or alcohol can be a dangerous cop-out, or flight from reality, rather than a serious means to go deeper into reality. They are a serious temptation—there is much anxiety in life, and we look for quick relief in many ways. What is quick and hurried is often violent, and non-lasting. Meditation is slow and gentle, and has permanent effects.

A final obstacle is the great desire we all have to control our lives, our situations, and even the lives of others when possible. We continually work to alter, change, fix, improve. This is really treating other people and the universe as objects for us to work on, rather than as living, sensitive beings and persons. Meditation means letting go of controls and letting ourselves and others ''just be''—what we are most reluctant to do.

Formal and Informal Meditation

From what we have said, we can see that meditation is a process of deepening our consciousness that goes on all during life if we are growing persons. Sometimes we hardly advert to these special moments of awareness. At other times they come to us spontaneously in a way that leaves an indelible impression. This could be a beautiful sunrise or sunset, the chirping of a bird in a forest, the sight of a friend, a deep impression during a symphony. It could be a time when we feel the great oneness in the universe, and the power and love of God that makes it possible. This is what we call informal or spontaneous meditation.

Formal meditation means to deliberately set aside some time or times during the day when we will devote ourselves to increasing our awareness and move to deeper levels. It means setting aside *prime time* when other occupations are put aside for a definite period. If we do so, we should not make the claim that we are ''meditators.'' The best meditation is that which moves along in every life situation. So there are some dangers in formal meditation. It is really a ''crutch'' to help us reach a time when we will not need special periods set aside, because our whole life has become meditative. However, most of us need crutches from time to time. In addition, the practice of daily formal meditation can be a help to make all of our life meditative—provided we do not make it a substitute for this.

The ''Goals'' of Meditation— The Levels at Which We Live

I have placed the word ''goals'' in quotations because meditation does not really have a goal outside of itself. Consciousness and awareness are really goals in themselves. In fact, if we look for some particular happening, such as a mystical experience or some kind of ''enlightenment,'' we may place an obstacle in the path of awareness by becoming object-oriented or utilitarian. However, in meditation, we move freely between the different levels in which we exist and act. I would like now to describe these levels. They apply to both formal and informal meditation.

1. *The Security or Survival Level.* Some of this is natural and physical—anxiety to preserve ourselves from death or injury; the need for food, drink, shelter and the basics of life. Or it can be artificial and acquired, *something that we have grown to equate with physical necessities or survival;* the uptightness that results from not having alcohol, drugs, a cigarette. Or it may be a fixed model or image of ourselves in our minds that we feel we must be, or else we become very upset—for example, to be a certain weight, or size, or figure, or to have certain qualities that would make ourselves acceptable to others.

2. *The Sensory Pleasure or Sensation Level.* Characteristic of this level is a concern to obtain and enjoy the pleasures of our senses, such as those that come from food, sex, and many other kinds of pleasurable sensation. These are part of life itself. It would be hard to imagine people who could not enjoy the pleasures of a good meal and the physical sensations of touch and sex.

3. *The Level of Mastery, Power or Order.* In this level we are concerned to control or master our own bodies and the situations in which we live, so that they may be to our advantage.

A note on these levels—it would not be right to call these imperfect or "lower levels." They are parts of every human existence. However, there are dangers in being "stuck" in any particular level. The following are signs that we have become "hung up" in one of them: when we become very upset, anxious, and separated from others by overconcern about the needs of any level; when other persons become mere objects to satisfy them—for example, if another person becomes a "sex-object," in the sensory level, or if in the power level, we try to dominate and control other people's lives in order to advance ourselves. We will say more about this later, but here we can note that meditation enables us to move freely to *all our levels* of consciousness and not become stuck in these first three levels.

4. *The Level of Care, Concern, and Love of Others.* In this level, we move away from purely personal concerns to love, care and service of others. We go out to others, not because they fulfill some need-se-

curity, pleasure, or power; this would be a ''conditional'' love, that is ultimately a self-love. It would be regarding others as objects. On the contrary, on this level we accept others unconditionally as they are in themselves, not because they fulfill a particular need we have of them or a model in our minds as to how they should be.

5. *The Level of Awareness and Consciousness.* In this level, we are able to watch our own life as if watching a drama in which you are the principal actor, the director, as well as the audience. You can see yourself in any of the above levels, watch and enjoy the show. You see yourself, your actions, your life pass by as if you are observing the clouds going by in the sky. You are deeply conscious and aware of life and all that is happening to you.

6. *The Level of Unity and Oneness.* At this level we have a deep, peaceful feeling of oneness and unity with all of the universe, with all other people, with plants, animals, all of nature, the sun, the planets, the stars, all of the universe in every form and energy. You no longer feel: ''Here I am, and there outside is the world.'' You tend to say, and feel, ''I am the world.''

In all the above levels, we have not mentioned God. This is because, as we shall see in Chapter 4, the God-nature in us is the Holy Spirit, literally ''the Holy Breath of God,'' the source of all life. This is not a separate part of us, but intimately a part of all human life and activity. Each of the above actually brings out one dimension of the Spirit as affecting one aspect of our existence and nature. In level 1, it is our bodily life existence itself, as made possible by the Spirit. In level 2, it is our emotions and feelings, likewise infused by the Spirit. In level 3, it is our minds that order and control, corresponding to the attribute of power belonging to God, the Holy Spirit. In level 4, it is really what we call the soul, our highest self. What comes from our highest self is characterized by the highest values such as love and concern for others. It is the most directly touched by the Holy Spirit, for the very essence of God is love: ''Beloved, let us love one another because love is of God'' (1 Jn 4:7). In level 5, we exercise the Godlike quality of being able to watch both ourselves and all of life as a great drama, fully conscious of all that is going on. In level 6, we experience to the fullest extent the one deep reality of the Spirit pervading the universe as bringing ourselves and all of mankind and nature together.

So if we may use the word "goals" of meditation, it is to explore the vast dimensions of our own existence that is so linked to the Spirit of God and to all other beings in the universe. This is impossible to do if we just look outside, for it becomes an endless quest. It is an "easy" task, if we *look inside,* for we *have everything we need.*

Some Basic Approaches in Formal Meditation

Later on we will deal with specific suggestions, such as the use of prayer, mantras, and various exercises. Here we will only deal with some approaches and suggestions that may help us to increase our awareness and move to deeper levels of our existence.

1. A basic "sitting meditation," for increased awareness

• Sit either on a chair, or on the ground using a pillow and crossing your legs. Keep your spine straight and erect. If on a chair, do not use the back support unless necessary. Focus your eyes gently in a particular area, but not on just one spot, to avoid a hypnotic effect.

• Have a quiet place set aside for your meditation.

• Give your attention to your sitting or posture and/or your breathing. As your body becomes centered and quiet, your mind will tend in the same direction.

• Let your attitude be that of an observer. Watch your thoughts and feelings come and go. Gently give each its proper attention. Let your attitude be that of the mother of a dozen children who gives enough attention to each but does not get stuck with each one. Watch yourself and your life go by as clouds in the sky, or as if you are sitting by a stream and watching the water flow.

• If anger, anxiety or other upsetting emotion comes to you, do not fight it but experience it fully as part of you. Then pass on. Later we will show how to use such emotions as ways to grow.

• Start with five minutes and gradually increase until you have a comfortable time set aside at least once a day for this exercise.

2. A basic walking meditation

Rarely we "just walk" and recover the joys we had when we took our first steps as a child.

• Concentrate your attention on your breathing and your walking. A good method is to put your steps in rhythm with your breath. Feel the weight of your feet as you lift them and put them on the ground. Walk slower than your usual pace. Feel the ground under your feet (barefoot helps!) and the feeling of pressure change as your foot goes to the ground and then leaves it.

3. Amidst ordinary activities

• Do things just a little differently. For example, let your bodily motions be less hurried. Brush your teeth with care and concern. Change your wristwatch to your other hand. If you are driving, listen to your car. Feel its vibrations, hear its motor, identify with it. The idea is to recover the spontaneous in life, where the automatic has come in to stifle insight and feeling. Make use of the many involuntary "stops" you have during the day—even welcome them as opportunities to center yourself, pray and meditate: a long traffic light, waiting for someone else, a delay, an interruption, even going to the bathroom.

Points for group or class discussion or personal reflection:

1. What are the biblical roots for the importance of the listening quality of meditation? How do you react to them?

2. What are the principal obstacles to meditation that you have found in your daily life? What would be ways to overcome them?

3. Give examples from your life or situations in which you have found yourself immersed in each of the following levels: (a) security, or survival, (b) sensation or pleasure, (c) power or control, (d) loving care of others, (e) awareness or consciousness, (f) unity and oneness.

4. What ways have you found helpful to provide time for reflection or meditation each day?

Annotated Bibliography for Further Reading

Nouwen, H., *Out of Silence* (Notre Dame, Ind.: Ave Maria, 1974). The author is well known for his books on how to meditate and cultivate an interior life.

Suzuki, S., *Zen Mind, Beginners Mind* (N.Y.: J. Weatherhill, 1970). A very practical guide for someone beginning Zen-type meditation as a path to personal awareness.

3

The Inner Source of Energy:
The Spirit/Breath of the Universe

In recent years the word "burn-out" (though still not in many dictionaries) has become very popular. A popular assumption is that we all have a limited supply of personal energy. Consequently, when this is used up through job stress, personal crises or other causes, we are almost helpless. Advertisements often prescribe various remedies such as workshops, counseling, diet, etc., to help people through this time. In contrast, Moses in the Bible was deeply moved when he first saw a burning bush that was not being burnt out or consumed (Ex 3:2). It meant that God was an inexhaustible source of energy and that Moses could be privileged to share and partake of this energy. No longer would there be any "burn-out" for him.

In our modern scientific world, every educated person knows (intellectually) that we live in an energy-filled universe. Every school boy or girl soon learns the formula of Einstein ($E = MC^2$) which shows that all matter is completely convertible with energy. The wonders of nuclear energy along with the terrible threat of nuclear annihilation have made us acutely aware of the enormous amount of energy stored in even a teaspoonful of water. However, what we know intellectually, the ancient biblical world knew in a very feeling way. They were convinced that all the universe was filled with divine energy that affected every moment of their lives. For them, this meant that there was an inner oneness in the universe by which all beings were interconnected. This divine energy at the source of all life was what they called the Spirit.

The term Spirit comes from the word "breath" not just in terms of physical intake of air, but in the sense of the vital energy present everywhere in the universe. In the biblical world, Spirit was a way of designating God as manifest in all creation, especially as life-energy. Since this Spirit is at the heart of our being, we can call upon it and tap it to bring a new source of strength to our quest for personal growth. It can give us a new source of confidence, when we become convinced that we *have within us all that we need.*

Most people tend to *look outside* for happiness in life whether in the form of money, power, prestige, sex, things, objects, or even other people. This does not mean that we cannot *prefer* to have many of these desirable additions to life. However, they are additions, nothing more. They are not the essence of life, happiness and growth which lie within us.

But is not God outside of us? It is the consistent biblical teaching in the Judeo-Christian tradition that God is not far from each one of us. In fact, he is nearer to us than we even dare imagine. This is because he is as near to us as life itself, and that is just about as near as we can get! When Paul arrived at Athens in the first century, he found an altar dedicated to the "Unknown God." This prompted him to affirm to the crowds: "He himself gives to all people life and breath and everything," and also: "He is not far from each one of us. 'In him we live and move and have our being' " (Acts 17:25, 28).

To understand the meaning of Spirit, the best place to start is with the biblical account of the creation of the world in Genesis 1—3. Everything starts with the mighty *ruah* of God (spirit or wind in Hebrew) sweeping over the uncontrolled oceans and waters that covered the earth. As God proceeds to create the plants, animals, and finally man, they are not made as if objects separate from himself. To the contrary, God places something of himself in each of them. In fact, he shares something intimate to his own nature—his creative power itself. First the earth is commanded and given the power to produce every kind of plant, tree and vegetation. Then each plant and tree is given the power to reproduce itself (1:11–12). Then the mighty sea is given the command to teem with an abundance of every kind of living creatures and fish (1:20). These in turn share God's creative power as he tells them, "Be fertile, multiply, and fill the water of the seas; and let the birds multiply on the earth" (1:22). The same powers are given to the animals. Finally man and woman are created to God's own image and likeness: "God created man and woman in his image; in the divine image he created them: male and female he created them" (Gen 1:27). The reference to male and female indicates two ways that we have divine elements within us. First it is a share in the creative power of God himself, as the text continues, "God blessed them, saying: 'Be fruitful and multiply; fill the earth and subdue it.'" The second is the ability like that of God to go out of one's self into relationships with others, especially in the form of friendship or marriage. In the Bible, the very essence of God is described in two qualities: *hesed,* meaning covenant love, and *emet,* meaning fidelity (cf. Ex 34:6). Finally human beings are made to the image of God because God has placed within them his own great power and mastery of the universe: "Have dominion over the fish of the sea, and over the birds of the air, and over every living thing that moves on the earth" (1:28).

As if this were not enough to show our inner resemblance to God himself, the Bible describes creation in this way, "The Lord God formed man out of dust from the ground and breathed into his nostrils the breath of life, and so man became a living being" (2:7). This is meant to show that the inner source of the life within us is no less than God himself. It is a share of God's own life. It is literally his holy breath—another way of saying his Holy Spirit. It is literally true, then, that we have this divine element within us. Because of this inner divine life, the Bible describes human life as the Spirit of God dwelling or remaining within us (Gen 6:3).

In contrast, the Bible describes death as a withdrawal of the divine Spirit. For example in Genesis 6:3, God says, "My Spirit shall not abide in man forever, for he is flesh, but his days shall be a hundred and twenty years." The word Spirit (breath) is found about eight hundred times in the Bible. This is a strong indication that ancient people were very aware of their breath and the breathing process. This awareness was a very important way to remember God's presence and draw strength from it.

It is interesting to note that all the world's great religions have recommended awareness of breathing as an important factor in meditation. It is well known that breathing concentration helps to promote the necessary relaxation needed for us to come in contact with powerful images lying deep in the unconscious. It is quite remarkable that the prophet Elisha almost three thousand years ago recognized the amazing energy process in breathing. He restored a young man to life by placing his own mouth on the mouth of the boy and breathing into him until he revived (2 Kgs 4:34–37). It is only in relatively modern times that this ancient method has been taken up again in mouth-to-mouth resuscitation.

The Holy Spirit or holy breath of God is not a static fixed element within us. It is meant to continually grow, move, and permeate our whole being as well as that of every person and creature in the universe. That is why the Bible is filled with references to a future great outpouring of the Holy Spirit. For example, the prophet Joel foretold, "It shall come to pass afterward that I will pour out my spirit upon all flesh. Your sons and daughters shall prophesy, your old men shall dream dreams, your young men shall see visions; even upon the servants and the handmaids, in those days, I will pour out my spirit" (3:1–2). Ezekiel had declared, "A new heart I will give you, and a new spirit I will put within you; I will take out of your flesh the heart of stone and give you a heart of flesh. I will put my spirit within you" (36:26–27). This future development of the Holy Spirit within us is often called the *messianic* Spirit because of the special place that a king or great agent of God will have in making this a complete reality. His special gift of the Spirit will enable others also to partake of it in an even deeper way. Thus Isaiah the prophet writes, "The Spirit of the Lord shall rest upon him: the spirit of wisdom and understanding, the spirit of counsel and might, the spirit of knowledge, and of fear of the Lord" (11:2–3).

At the Jordan, when Jesus saw the Spirit coming upon him in the form of a dove and resting upon him, he felt that he was the one to fulfill the promise of Isaiah and make possible a great outpouring of the Holy Spirit. In the Gospel of John, John the Baptist gives this testimony: "He who sent me to baptize with water said to me, 'He on whom you see the Spirit descend and remain on someone, this is he who baptizes with the Holy Spirit' " (1:33). The early Church felt that Jesus had the full breath or Spirit of God and that he shared this with them. This was confirmed to them on the evening of Easter Sunday when they were assembled together behind closed doors. Jesus appeared to them, identified himself, and greeted them with the words, "Peace be with you." To understand what Jesus did next, we must recall the creation account in Genesis where God breathed upon the first man and woman and shared his own life or Spirit with them. Jesus likewise breathed on his disciples, to show that he had the fullness of the breath of God which is to be shared with us (Jn 20:22). This Spirit of God is his very essence, for it is a Spirit of love, forgiveness, peace and reconciliation. This we see in Jesus' next words, "If you forgive the sins of any, they are forgiven" (20:23).

The implications of what we have been saying are so startling that we should take some time to absorb what they mean:

1. We need only to *look inside* to experience that *we have all we really need within.* What more could be needed than the Holy Breath of God—the Holy Spirit!
2. When we are conscious of this divine life within us, and really experience it, we are actually in tune with the whole heart of the universe. Alertness, consciousness, awareness is all that is needed.
3. There is an inner movement, direction, power and meaning in our life that we can find for ourselves, if we *look.*
4. Other creatures also have the same spark within them—plants, trees, animals, and all of nature according to their capacity. This leads us to a basic reverence and respect for all of life. In fact, each is in some way our superior because it manifests the divine spark in some unique way that no one else can duplicate. We are all *equals,* for our most precious gift is common to all, even though its manner of manifestation is different.
5. When we are together with other people, there is a certain fullness of the Spirit or presence of God that lends an exciting new dimension to life. Each of us is a precious jewel reflecting in a unique way the divine light within. The presence and friendship of other jewels presents a full spectrum or dimension that enhances our own gift as well as that of the whole group and each person also.
6. The creation account teaches us that love belongs to the very essence of God. Power is only one of his qualities. In fact, he is continually and voluntarily limiting his power by sharing all that he has with others. He is a God who "lets others be" and respects their choices. Love means to continually limit our power by pouring out what we have to others. It is the opposite of any kind of violence.
7. If there is one person, or one creature, or one animal, one plant in the universe that we do not love, then we do not love at all. Love is unconditional and goes to the essence of all being which is the divine light and spark within all.

Some parallels may give at least a partial picture of the tremendous realities we have been discussing. For example, everyone is familiar with electricity in its effects, but there are only theories about what it actually is in essence. We see its effects in a light bulb, a machine, a motor, a heating or refrigerating unit. Each "fixture" or appliance manifests the inner electricity in some special unique way, yet all are equal in the source. Is a light bulb greater than a motor? Or is one light bulb greater than another because it allows more electricity to flow? The two bulbs are equal because they give all the light they are meant to give; they perfectly fulfill their nature. It is impossible to make comparisons, or to judge. As we start making judgments and comparisons, we lose the consciousness and experience of the light within by dwelling in the prison of our minds.

Another parallel is that of a master artist with a studio filled with works of art in various stages of completion. The artist gradually works on the different pieces according to his or her inspiration. One work may take years to complete; another may take days. However, *each is at the stage where it should be at this time*. A picture that has been years in the making may be suddenly completed by a few brilliant strokes of the artist. All the masterpieces *together* bring out the genius of the Creator, but each in some unique way. This is how God works. The important matter is that we grow and are ready for the touch of the Master.

As a consequence of all this, we can confidently state:

• Love and violence are opposed to one another. Life can be given as an outpouring of self, but it cannot be taken away. This applies not only to human beings, but even to plants, trees and animals. Note that Genesis 1:29–30 has God saying to man and the animals: ''Behold I have given you every plant-yielding seed which is upon the face of the earth and every tree with seed in its fruit; you shall have them for food. And to every beast of the earth and to every bird of the air, and to everything that creeps on the ground, I have given every green plant for food.'' Such is the extreme and delicate reverence for life that even the green plants are a *gift* of life from God that must be reverenced. Our attitude, even while eating vegetables, should be that of grateful reception of life from God, and not a taking away of life. In fact, in the early Genesis account the writer does not see even animals as killing other animals for meat. The prophet Isaiah presents an idyllic picture of a peaceful world where even the animals do not resort to violence: ''The wolf shall dwell with the lamb, and the leopard shall lie down with the kid; the calf and the young lion and the fatling together and a little child to guide them'' (11:6–7). In the Book of Genesis, permission to kill animals for meat appears to be given later and with some reluctance: ''Every moving thing that lives shall be good for you; and as I gave you the green plants, I give you everything'' (9:3). Here once again it is the matter of a gift. The fish or animal we eat should be regarded with reverence as one who has given its life that you may live.

Exercises

One of the secrets of fruitful meditation lies in your breath itself, especially in the depth of meaning that we have just described. It should be noted also that it is one of the few bodily functions that can be either deliberate or automatic (during our sleep or when we are not conscious of our breathing). Concentration on breathing is so important because it helps us to become conscious of life itself and its Source. In addition, when we concentrate on our breath, we cannot give attention to anything else. As soon as we do, we lose our concentration.

Try the following exercises:

1. Sit still, either on the ground with legs crossed, or in a chair with spine erect, preferably without a back support. This is a help to promote alertness and to center ourselves. When our body is centered, our whole being tends to be centered. Gently *watch* your breathing. Do not try to control it, accelerate it or slow it down, or take deep or shallow breaths. Try to feel your breath fully during the whole cycle from the time it enters your nostrils to the time it reaches the depths of your lungs and comes out again. See if you can count twenty breaths in this fashion. If you can, no need to seek a guru in the Himalayas—you are there!

2. Close your eyes and go back to the first moments after you came from your mother's womb—when you cried and took your first breaths of fresh air after being nine months under water. By conscious breathing, experience fully the first ten breaths of your life as a beautiful gift of God's own life. *Accept* your life, and choose to live it in order to love and serve others.

3. Imagine the scene described in Genesis 2:7 where God breathes his own Spirit into the first man and woman. Imagine that you are Adam or Eve (who really represent all men and women). Be aware of your respiration and consciously take in the Holy Spirit of God with each breath. Use the mantra (silently) "Come, Holy Spirit," each time you breathe in. As you feel more and more energy within you, consciously breathe

out and with the outbreath send this energy to people or situations where this energy is very much needed.

Points for group or class discussion or personal reflection:

1. Describe some situation in which you or someone you know has experienced "burn-out." Then suggest how this chapter could be practically applied to prevent this from happening again.

2. How can meditative breathing be used (A) to bring about inner calm, (B) as a way of prayer, (C) as a way to heal ourselves and others?

3. With a stopwatch or second hand, time yourself for one minute as you watch your breathing and count it. How many breaths did you take in sixty seconds? What experiences did you have at this time? Figure out how many breaths you take in an hour, in a day. What significance does this have for you?

Annotated Bibliography For Further Reading

DeMello, Anthony, *Sadhana: A Way to God: Christian Exercises in Eastern Form* (St. Louis, Mo.: Institute of Jesuit Studies, 1974). The eastern use of breathing and other meditative approaches are explained in a Christian context.

Montague, G.T., *The Holy Spirit: Growth of a Biblical Tradition* (Ramsey, N.J.: Paulist, 1976). A very fine biblical understanding of the Spirit by a well-known Scripture scholar familiar with the charismatic movement.

4

How To Consult
Your Inner Guide

The Spirit, the Soul and the Inner Guide

The Spirit/Breath is the source of all life in the universe. Yet each one of us is an independent breathing, living being. The Bible calls this in Hebrew the *nefesh* which was translated in the Greek Bible as *psyche,* usually rendered in English by the word "soul" or living being. The earlier biblical view of soul was not that of a separated immortal part of us enclosed in a bodily frame. This is a later Greek-influenced view. In contrast, the earlier biblical books considered our whole bodily existence in all its parts as suffused with the life principle. Modern biological science supports the view that all of life is in every cell of the human body: that our human life is *all in one and one in all.*

This view, interestingly enough, conforms to the old view of the soul in Scholastic philosophy, namely, that the soul is not a separate part of us, but located in its entirety in every area of the human body. In these pages, we will refer the soul as the Self, to distinguish it from the self, which we will use to designate the will, or center of voluntary operation.

How are the Spirit (which we will often designate as the SELF—all caps) and the Self, or soul, to be distinguished? Actually they cannot be neatly dissevered since the ultimate source of life, the Spirit, can never be separated from any living being. Yet each one of us is an individuated unique living being. Thus we may designate our most intimate connection to the Spirit, the source of all life, as the "soul" or Self. This latter is the "mediator" of the Spirit, the point through which the great divine Spirit operates. The Bible uses the term "my spirit" or "your spirit" to designate this individuated source of life. Sometimes "my spirit" is written in parallel with "soul" or living being. Mary, the mother of Jesus, for example says, "My soul (*psyche*) magnifies the Lord and my spirit rejoices in God my Savior (Lk 1:46).

Consequently, Spirit and soul are mysteriously intertwined and interconnected, the soul being the "mediator" or closest link to the Spirit in our bodily existence. So when we refer to the Inner Guide, we mean ultimately the Holy Spirit but mediately the soul or highest Self. In the process of personal integration, the highest Self plays the essential role, both by its energy and by its direction. The will or self is also very important, but it is more an instrument that can be used both for good and for evil. In contrast, the action of the highest Self, or soul, is always characterized by the highest good for both individual and community. It leads to actions that are prompted by the most lofty ethical values and by loving service to others. It promotes oneness between human beings in relationship and in community. Actions moved by the Self have a characteristic broadness and expansiveness about them. Because of its intimate connection with the Spirit, the soul or highest Self is immortal. The work of individuation accomplished by the Spirit in each human person is everlasting. This is why Jesus could quote the Scriptures and call his Father the "God of Abraham, the God of Isaac and the God of Jacob" (Mt 22:32). When we refer to the Inner Guide in this work it can often mean either the Holy Spirit, the highest Self, or both since they are so intimately connected.

Getting in Touch with the Inner Guide

More and more people of today resort to counselors in time of stress and special difficulty. External consultation is often a symbol of an inner journey to seek guidance from an inner guide, deep within. In biblical times, people quite naturally went to consult God for answers and guidance. For example, at one time Rebecca, the wife of Isaac, was quite disturbed because of the excessive movement of the twins within her womb. The biblical text simply says that she went to consult the Lord, and he said to her:

> Two nations are in your womb,
> and two peoples born of you shall be divided.
> But one shall be stronger than the other;
> the elder shall serve the younger (Gen 25:23).

The text does not describe how she consulted God, but other passages indicate that people consulted God through a seer, priest, prophet or gifted person through whom God spoke. When Saul sought advice on how to find the lost donkeys of his father, he went to Samuel the seer and prophet (1 Sam 9). When Saul became king, the whole country was under the domination of the Philistines. These coastal people knew how to forge iron and were armed with iron swords, spears and armored chariots, while the Israelites had only wooden clubs and weapons. King Saul was faced with a crisis when his son Jonathan, with only a few men, surprised a Philistine fort. Should he initiate an attack on the Philistines despite the overwhelming obstacles against them? To decide the matter, he consulted God through a priest (1 Sam 14:18–20).

Here we find more details as to how this was done. The text notes that the priest was wearing an *ephod*. This was a burse containing sacred lots that the priest wore in front of his chest. Saul told him to put his hand in the ephod and withdraw (the lot) to look for a "yes" or "no" answer as to whether he should attack the Philistines. The answer was "yes," since the people gave a great shout and went ahead with the attack. The priests of that day always carried these divine lots called the *urim* and *thummim* during worship so they could always be ready to provide consultation with God for the people.

Such belief in consultation was not limited to the Old Testament. In the New Testament we find similar trust in consultation when it comes to the choice of a new twelfth apostle to take the place of Judas the betrayer who had taken his life. The first Christians proposed two names, then prayed and cast lots to see which one should be chosen. The choice fell on Matthias (Acts 1:23–26).

What is all this based upon? It is founded on the belief that there is an inner divine movement behind events and history. Things do not happen by mere chance. It was also believed that it was possible at times for gifted men and women to obtain an insight as to what this hidden plan and direction was. For Christians, the supreme Counselor and Guide is the Holy Spirit. It has been customary for the Church and individual Christians over many centuries to seek guidance from the Holy Spirit in all important matters. This Holy Spirit, the Holy Breath of God, is not far off, but deep within us. It is important then to know how to ask for inner guidance and be able to follow its directions.

First of all, valuable guidance and direction comes to us when we really listen to the meaning of the events of life. Behind the external happening is an inner divine movement that has a special meaning for our lives. Jesus called attention to this when he asked what meaning the death of Galilean revolutionaries and the accidental deaths of people killed by a falling tower had for the people of his time (Lk 13:1–5).

Second, at times this inner direction behind human events can erupt through dreams. When Paul the apostle was deliberating about whether to begin a missionary journey to Greece and Europe, he had a vision in a dream, in which a man from Macedonia stood beside him and invited him to come to Greece with the words, ''Come over to Macedonia and help us'' (Acts 16:9). Paul took this as a message from God. Luke writes, ''After this vision, we immediately sought to go on into Macedonia, concluding that God had called us to preach the good news to them'' (16:10). We will treat specifically of dreams in the following section.

Finally, the supreme method of seeking guidance is through prayer. The biblical way to stress this is through constant repetition using new images each time. Thus in Matthew 7: 7–8 Jesus uses a threefold parallel repeated twice to make it absolutely certain how important this message is:

Ask, and you will receive.	For the one who asks, receives.
Seek, and you will find.	The one who seeks, finds.
Knock, and it will be opened to you.	The one who knocks, enters.

Exercises and Practice

1. Think of some pressing problem for which you need an answer or solution. Then concentrate on your breathing. Count ten breaths, trying to feel them as deeply as possible. Now go to the principle of breath and life, the Holy Spirit, and with each breath say the words on the in-breath, ''Come, Holy Spirit,'' and on the out-breath, ''Guide us in your love.'' Do this ten times. Then recall the problem or question you previously selected. Take in the question with your in-breath, then let an answer go out through your out-breath. Repeat this a number of times until you feel at peace about it.

2. After reading the daily newspaper or watching the news on TV, look over the headlines and recall the principal events. Then ask yourself, ''What does this event mean in my life?'' Wait for an answer.

3. (Alone or with a group) Place a lighted candle in the center of a room darkened as much as possible. Carefully study the candle and its details. Then close your eyes and check how well you can imagine the flame. Then open your eyes and see what details you have missed. Repeat the process, opening and closing your eyes until you have a sharp internal image of the flame. Now keep your eyes closed and imagine that you see the figure of Jesus or someone you feel is a person of great wisdom. Then ask Jesus or that person about a problem, a question that you have been trying to decide. Look for an answer either by word, gesture or image of some kind. Ask also about anything else you may wish to discuss and then await an answer.

Notes on This Exercise

A. If you do not receive an answer, it may be that the time is not yet ripe for it. Often an answer comes simply in the assurance or confidence that we feel.

B The exercise is a way (through images) to enter into dialogue with the Holy Spirit or our inner wisdom guide in the center of our soul. It can be used in times of decision or even daily. Answers or dialogue may be recorded in our daily journal (cf. last chapter).

C. We can always trust the counsel given us by the Holy Spirit or our Inner Guide. Sometimes, however, we may not be sure about whether it comes from this source. How are we to know the difference and exercise ''discretion of spirits''? We have some criteria from the New Testament to help us. Characteristic of the Holy Spirit is God's own love and concern for others. ''God's love has been poured out in our hearts through the Holy Spirit who has been given to us'' (Rom 5:5). In addition, a sign of the guidance of the Holy Spirit is a deep sense of values and ethical concerns. What comes from the Holy Spirit builds up both ourselves, others and the whole community: ''To each is given the manifestation of the Spirit for the common good'' (1 Cor 12:7).

There is also an important indirect way the Holy Spirit speaks to us.

Christian tradition has always advised the selection of a spiritual counselor or guide. Yet a word of warning must be offered. Today there is a great abundance of gurus, counselors and guides who establish a clientele around them. The New Testament insists that our Inner Guide is the Holy Spirit and warns against merely human discipleship. In Matthew 23:10 Jesus says, "Neither be called teachers. Only one is your teacher, the Messiah." The author of the First Letter of John writes, "You have no need that anyone should teach you, as his anointing teaches you about everything" (2:27). These texts warn us to listen to the Holy Spirit and not be dependent on merely human guides. Yet at the same time, the Holy Spirit speaks not only from our own hearts but through other people. And in people, the Spirit speaks especially through holy men and women. Often the Spirit works through both ourselves and others at the same time. In other words, our journey to see a spiritual advisor is symbolic of our inner journey to seek our spiritual guide within. And in our dialogue with a spiritual counselor we can enter into dialogue with our Inner Guide, the Spirit.

It is important to discuss the qualifications of such a guide. It should be someone who conforms to the model of Jesus by having his or her priorities in life as the kingdom of God which means a world of peace and justice. A second criterion is that our guide should be a person who is a man or woman of prayer. Third, it should be someone who has knowledge—knowledge of the Scriptures and the tradition of great religious teachers. Yet not all people with these characteristics would be good spiritual guides. It is important that we find someone who can really listen to us and understand us. In other words, our spiritual guide is really a friend who can speak to us as an equal on our own level. It should be a person really and genuinely concerned about us and our spiritual progress. The goal of a true guide is to draw us closer to God and help us to be free and independent—even of the best of teachers.

Another important method of consultation is to listen to the message that our dreams send to us. But, first, we must know the language of our dreams.

The Language of Dreams

Most of us spend approximately one-third of our life on our backs, resting in bed. We know well the physical effect of sleep on our bodies, yet the psychological effects are mysterious and still under exploration. During our sleep all of us dream at one time or another. Sometimes they are vivid and remembered for years; at other times there is but a hazy memory of something that has been dimly a part of our experience. More and more it is being understood that dreams play an essential part in the whole process of growth and integration. This part can be greatly enhanced if we give better attention to our dreams and their meaning.

There are two main types of dreams. The first and most common type of dream deals with the deeper meaning as well as emotional impact of the events of each day. We pass rapidly through life and often are unable, for various reasons, to experience the full emotional meaning and impact of the events of each day. The experience is similar to the one we have on gazing at a snapshot taken perhaps at a speed of 1/50 or 1/100 of a second until we can absorb its full meaning and impact. During life we are continually taking snapshots that will later be left to our dreams for further observation. We could not possibly absorb their full meaning in our waking time. It is helpful when we are awake to go through such dreams at leisure so we can fully absorb their import and meaning.

The second is even more important, but rarer. It is the dream that brings us deep into the common experience of ourselves and others in the universe. These are dreams that give us important insights about the past, present and especially the future. The renowned psychotherapist, Carl Jung, called these the dreams that bring us into the great universal and cosmic archetypes. Through them we can deeply penetrate into the common experience of the whole human race. In the Bible we find a number of examples of such dreams. For example, in Matthew 2, Joseph is warned in a dream to bring Mary and the child Jesus into Egypt that very night because Herod the king was seeking to kill the child.

The Structure of Dreams

A dream is like a stage play. We direct it from some deep mysterious place within. We also compose the script. The actors are the various parts of our being. If, for example, someone dies in a dream, it is some part of our personality that has died, or is dying. We are also the audience of the stage play, to whom the meaning and message is directed.

Language of Dreams

Since we are the composers of our dreams, their meaning is known at some point within our personality. Yet dreams usually do not communicate in the same way as we do in our awakened state. Dreams usually communicate by pictures or images that have a symbolic content. Yet it is not possible to nicely catalogue these images and their meaning. Two people can have the same dream but with distinct shades of meaning for them. No one else can possibly interpret or tell us the meaning of our dreams. At most they can facilitate the process by asking questions and helping us as we search for the special message we ourselves have composed. The meaning of a dream is recovered only when the person has the insight that some interpretation feels comfortable and fits his or her own life situation.

Some Hints on the Use of Dreams
in the Personal Growth Process

First of all, not all dreams are of equal value. The more vivid and impressive dreams occur during times of crisis in life. Repeated dreams are literally clamoring for our attention. Then, too, each person is different. Dreams may be much more important and expressive in one person than in another who may be growing rapidly through other processes and thus has less or no need of dreams. Again, dreams will not yield all their secrets unless we give them attention. A person who dreams, but always forgets them, may find that all that is needed is to make a definite effort to remember them and realize their importance. It is quite important, then, to spend time each day in absorbing the meaning of our dreams. To this end, it is helpful to take down notes on our dreams in our journal, as we will describe in our last chapter. Talking them over with a spouse or friend is also an important help. In trying to get to their meaning, we repeat again that the important key is what best fits our life situation.

In the process of analysis, look at the different actors or people in the dream. Try to discover which parts of you they represent, what they are saying to each other and to you the audience. If there is a death in your dream, see which part of you is dying. This is not a cause of concern—it can mean that new life is about to burst forth. If you have trouble trying to recover the meaning of a dream, be patient. Its message will come through when you are ready for it. The following method is often helpful. Close your eyes, and in fantasy recover the scene, images and dialogue of your dream. If there is some symbol or person or dialogue you do not understand, *ask* what it means and wait for an answer. If it does not come, it means that somehow the time is not ripe for it.

Points for group or class discussion or personal reflection:

1. How is the Spirit related to the soul and will? What consequences does this have for personal growth?

2. Describe various ways we can contact our Inner Guide. Are there any other ways that you have found helpful? What are the ''rules'' for ''discretion of spirits''?

3. What part do dreams play in life? How can we interpret their meaning in reference to our growth process?

Annotated Bibliography for Further Reading

Assagioli, R., *Psychosynthesis* (N.Y.: Viking, 1971). An important reference book for the process of psychosynthesis that places special emphasis on the inner guidance of the highest Self or soul.

Fischer, K.R., *The Inner Rainbow* (Ramsey, N.J.: Paulist, 1983). This book is a valuable guide toward using images in prayer, faith, spirituality and reading the Scriptures.

Savary, M., Berne, P., Williams, S., *Dreams and Spiritual Growth* (Ramsey, N.J.: Paulist, 1984). Combines a psychological and spiritual approach to working with dreams for personal growth.

5

The Skillful Will,
the Instrument of Change

Before any real progress in personal growth can be made, there is one step that must be taken. It is a hard and difficult one, but absolutely necessary. This step is a clear, unconditional acceptance of responsibility for one's own life—actions, feelings and experience. This sounds simple, but most people go through life blaming other people or life situations for their anger, sorrow, frustration or lack of progress. How often do we not hear expressions such as this: "If only I had a different job or boss, things would be different," or "If I had more money, I would be happy." The list is long—parents, education, opportunities, environment, heredity, culture, etc. Much of this blaming is an escape from responsibility—an *unwill*ingness or fear to use our *will* to influence the course of our life.

First of all, what are some of the obstacles to development of will power and responsible decision making? A realistic look at the world around us makes it appear difficult or almost impossible to effect change in ourselves and the outside world. We are heavily programmed by powerful outside influence. From the moment of birth and conception, the genes and chromosomes in our cells influence the whole course and direction our life is to take. Then our parents through their example, words and actions place in us powerful models of behavior. Beyond the family, radio, the newspaper and television bring into every home carefully prepared programming by billion dollar corporations to influence our thinking and life-styles in accord with the profit interests of a narrow, rich and powerful segment of the population. Government enters into every sphere of life and education. An unholy alliance of government with military and industrial complexes makes their influence almost irresistible.

In the face of all this what can a single person do to influence the world? All of this calls for a brief response at this point. The most powerful means of influence and communication is not mass media or any other form of control. The power of good is contagious as it flows from person to person—just as one person with the flu could give it to thousands within one day. All we need to do is to change the course of our own life, feelings and actions. The world will change with us. This is because the world is not an object out there. We are part of it. *We are the world,* as Krishnamurti is fond of saying. It is the will that can push on to the first step in transforming our lives.

Second, we often hear it said that life itself is the best teacher—that we need to "flow with life" and not resist the tide. This has a strong element of truth in it. We are not alone, but part of a great stream of life that is constantly teaching us through the events, happenings and personal encounters of each day. All of these have special meaning for us. At the same time, however, we are not helplessly caught in the "flow of life." We are actually part of it. As part of it we can play a surprisingly large part in directing the flow. It is a conscious flow, not a mechanical one. The development of our own life can have two effects: we can direct *our* part of the flow of life and, secondly, use all that comes to us in the rest of that flow not as obstacles but as challenges and opportunities to grow.

In succeeding units we will develop patterns to show how the will can effectively help us in personal growth. This will be first of all in the area of the entanglements, cravings and addictions that are the principal obstacle to personal growth. The will also prompts us to enter into personal relations with others and develop the responsibilities that friendship, love and marriage require. In addition, each person usually assumes some kind of more universal service to the world in the form of a job, career, or voluntary service. It is the will that directs the choice in this all-important area.

Limitations and Dangers vs. A Positive Approach

There are, however, limitations and dangers in the use of the will. We are well aware that many men and women in history have developed powerful wills and used them to control others and inflict incalculable evil on the world. Examples of Hitler, Mussolini and other political leaders quickly come to mind. The will is an instrument that can be used for good or for evil. It becomes evil when not properly integrated and at the service of higher faculties. When the will is integrated and at the service of the soul and the Spirit (cf. Chapter 4), the action of the will is dominated by love, ethical concerns and the highest values. Otherwise the will itself can become a slave of selfish, power-centered interest.

Another danger in the use of the will is to attempt to use the will as a mere instrument of force or coercion to drive our bodies as slaves to do things we could not ordinarily do. On the contrary, the skillful will directs more by gentle persuasion than as a slavemaster. It directs the body, feelings and mind in an accord with their needs and inclinations so that there is a harmonious compliance even in difficult matters. Without this, eventually there will be a breakdown or revolt as the human faculties refuse to follow a tyrant and slavedriver will.

The most effective way the will can be exercised is not directly but indirectly through images. In the last twenty years there has been a wealth of significant research on the dynamic effects of images on our personal formation and growth. These images are not pictures in our imagination but deep-seated, energy-packed emotional clusters that move and direct our lives. Some of these images can function as real roadblocks to growth: e.g., models, demands and expectations of what we *should be,* based on what other people ask of us. In Chapter 7, "Overcoming Entanglements and Roadblocks," we will see how the will can dissipate the destructive force of such images. In contrast, the powerful positive images representing the spirit, the highest Self and other integrating factors can supply us with unlimited energy and impetus to personal growth. The will can summon these indirectly through the use of guided fantasy, bodily movement, meditation and other ways. Throughout this book the will's use of images will be the most important factor in methodology for integration.

Hints for Developing a Skillful Will

1. Learn to make decisions effectively. Gather all the facts necessary. Ask for the opinions and advice of others. Weigh alternatives carefully. When sufficient evidence is gathered, act decisively without delay. Don't procrastinate. Postpone only if insufficient information is present.

2. Take responsibility for decisions you have made. Do not blame others or circumstances if things go wrong.

3. Be willing to risk and learn through mistakes. People "with experience" are those who have learned to profit from their errors. The precise accuracy of rockets and space travel is made possible by constant "correcting" of mistakes in course by checking positions.

4. Assume responsibility for your life and happiness. Don't be constantly blaming others when you feel anger or frustration. Look within for causes—more on this in coming chapters.

5. Take the risk of entering into human relationships whether love, friendship or marriage. Look upon these as a choice or responsibility that you will be faithful to despite human weakness and failure of ourselves or others. An enlightened will makes the choice of love unconditionally—out of a desire to give and share with others. A conditional love is prompted only by pleasure, self-interest or gain of some kind. When these factors disappear, the relationship breaks up.

Some Exercises for Developing and Strengthening the Will

1. Deliberately break routines. We all easily become "creatures of habit" and diminish the use of the will by eliminating choices in daily life. When this happens, a sudden unexpected event that involuntarily breaks our routine leaves us weak and helpless. Animals become trapped and die because skillful hunters find out their routines—when and where they water, feed or rest. We likewise become trapped and dead when we live a life of routine. A good way to use the will to break routine and thus strengthen it as well as open up new possibilities in life is through new choices. The regulation of the day into definite time periods—to eat, to work, to rest—is often helpful, but it can enslave us. For example, try to avoid using your wristwatch on some day, or change it to another wrist, or put it into your pocket. Make the choice to eat not at a fixed hour but at some other time or when you are really hungry. Make the choice to fast or give up a meal at certain times—using the savings perhaps to buy food for the hungry. These are only suggestions. There are countless ways, in time, clothes, activities, use of TV, radio, etc., where we can break the power of routine, develop the power of the will and open up new vistas in life.

2. Try the "I can't, I won't, I'll try" exercise. Make a list of, say,

ten things you would like to do, but feel you can't. Write, for example, "I would like to (e.g., travel to Europe, backpack in the mountains, etc.), but I feel I can't." Second, go through your list carefully and cross out "I feel I can't"; then change each expression to "I would like to" (as above) but I *won't* (unless it is an absolute impossibility such as a trip to the moon next week). See that it is your unwillingness to make the choice that stands in your way—your weak will. Third go through the list again, cross out "I won't" and write "I'll try"—then note a first step you will be taking, today if possible, to realize your desire. Keep this list and follow it up in your daily journal according to the process to be described at the end of the book. You will soon be surprised to see many of your former "dreams" soon become realities in your life. In the process you will gradually become more and more strengthened through opening up new dimensions and possibilities in your life. The word "impossible" will be found less and less in your vocabulary.

Points for group or class discussion or personal reflection:

1. Many people, often unconsciously, adopt a "behaviorist" view on life—that we are completely dominated by heredity, the surrounding cultural influences, environment, etc. To what extent is this true? Is it possible for a person to make a significant breakthrough despite these obstacles? What steps can be taken to do so?

2. What are the dangers involved in trying to accomplish things through sheer will power? Describe some world leaders who have used a strong will to accomplish good. Do the same in regard to historical figures who have used a powerful will toward evil ends.

3. What is the best way to develop a truly skillful will that will move us toward real spiritual and personal growth? What ways have you found helpful to do this? Give examples.

4. Make a list of significant ways that you can strengthen your will today and during the coming week.

6

The Will and
Integration Areas

Sub-Personalities

What is a person? The original meaning of the word is very revealing. The Latin root is from "per" (through) and "sonare" (to sound). The word *persona* was used of the different masks that an actor wore as he assumed different roles—the masks through which his voice resounded. In each of us, the person is really what is behind all the roles or masks of being or acting that we assume in daily life. These roles are not just parts we play or accidental externals. They correspond to something deep within us that can be exercised as the occasion demands. For example, I can be a teacher when communicating information to someone (a student) who comes to me for an answer. I can be a child at various times in my life. I am a man, a father, a lover, a writer, a dancer, a musician or artist and many others because all these qualities lie within me and can be made manifest to others at various times. We will call these roles or outward manifestations of the persona "sub-personalities." The sum total of them all is a valuable indication of the *persona* itself.

To further *persona* growth it is important to work with these sub-personalities. Many people get "stuck" on one or two of them and thus stunt the growth of others and even the whole person. For example, being a teacher is an important role or subpersonality in my life as a professional college teacher. However, I can give so much attention to this matter of being a teacher that I adopt a superior attitude that would hinder the equality needed to be a friend or a lover. I can thus hinder the use and development of other subpersonalities that would help me become a well-integrated person. In order to develop them, (1) I must first become aware and conscious of each of them, (2) I must be able to fully enter into and feel each one of them (association), (3) I must be able to step in and step out of these various sub-personalities so that I do not become stuck in any one of them (disassociation), (4) I must be able to develop the sub-surface underdeveloped s.p.'s so they will play their proper part in my personal growth. This means decreasing or placing in proper perspective the s.p.'s so they work harmoniously and strengthen one another as well as the whole personality.

Before we go any further, take a piece of paper and make a test of your own sub-personalities as they come to your mind. Number them 1, 2, 3, etc. If possible, give to each one an appropriate name to help promote identification and recognition, e.g., the dancer—"Dancing Dan"; the musician, "Beethoven or Mozart," etc. Then go along the list and note an s.p. that seems very evident to others and perhaps over developed and emphasized. Then go over the list and note one or two others that seem hidden and need to be more developed or come to the surface.

At this point let us try to get a picture of our goal in the form of two images. The first is that of a large diamond with an inner light and a many-faceted surface. Each facet glistens with a unique color and glow as it manifests some aspect of the inner light. The rays of light coming together from all the facets blend together giving a beautiful total effect of the light within. This is a picture of one whole personality (a diamond) made up of myriads of brilliant reflecting surfaces. Each facet contributes an important part to the whole diamond as well as to every other facet so that they blend harmoniously into the whole and form something beyond the power of each part or all the parts one by one. If any of the parts of the diamond are covered over or blurred, the whole diamond itself loses some of its brilliance and every other part suffers as well.

A second image is that of a symphony orchestra. If you arrive early, you hear the various instruments tune up, each with its unique sound. It is helpful to hear the individual instruments and identify them. Yet with each playing on one's own, the result is a rather disturbing noise. This is the picture of s.p.'s working together yet in disharmony so that the sounds of one counteract or conflict with those of others. Then suddenly the conductor steps in, tapping his or her stick. (This is the will.) The conductor lifts a baton and all begin to play, this time with a beautiful harmony. The sounds of the various players blend together, strengthening and balancing one another. At times the conductor signals for various instruments to amplify their contribution, silencing others or reducing their volume. The result of the oneness and harmony of so many people under the conductor makes for a beautiful work of art that vibrates in waves through the audience and through the universe. Behind the director (will) is the composer. The composer is the soul or highest self moving the will to perform the music so that it can be of loving service to all. Behind the composer is the Supreme Composer, God the Holy Spirit.

Sub-personalities cannot be discovered or developed except through active experience, so the exercises that follow are of key importance. They may be done alone or with someone leading a group.

1. The House of the Many Selves

In this exercise and in many through the book, we will make use of guided imagery. Images are not just ideas or mental pictures. They are thoughts that take flesh and influence our lives at deep levels. It is often impossible to reach these areas except through such images.

Exercise: Close your eyes. Give attention to your breathing as described in Chapters 1 and 2. Imagine that you are in a meadow. In the distance you see a house. You go up to it and look at the door. You decide to go in and explore the different rooms. In each room you discover one of your sub-personalities in some form—it might even be an animal or symbol. Take time to explore the house. When you finish, invite two of your s.p.'s to come outside with you—a dominant one and also one that is hidden or needs development. Give a name to each one of them. When they come out, enter into conversation with them. Ask both what they can give to you and what you can give to them. Then have the two s.p.'s enter into dialogue with each other, with the same questions posed to one another. Then discuss how all of you can work best together. Now bring your two friends into the direct sunlight and open up yourselves to its warmth and light. Watch and note whatever transformation takes place under the sun's rays. Finally when you are finished, open your eyes. If you are in a group, each can briefly share at least part of what happened during the meditation. If by yourself, note down briefly what happened to you during the guided fantasy.

Some notes on this exercise: The house is a frequent image of the self that comes up in dreams, fantasies, etc. The exploration of the rooms gives the opportunity to search and bring to light many hidden aspects of the self. We mention symbols, because this is an important way that our s.p.'s communicate to us. The unconscious has its own language. The dialogue furnishes the opportunity for the will to recognize the needs of the s.p.'s and to direct them so as to harmonize them with each other and the whole person. The sun is an ancient symbol of the highest self as well as God. If through the image the sun shines, it acts to strengthen the will as well as the s.p.'s. Transformation takes place under the sun's action as the s.p.'s learn to modify themselves and grow harmoniously. Writing down the experience gives the opportunity for further insights to arise as well as for recording for future use. The same is true of the verbal sharing. Both writing and oral sharing help in the important expression of the feeling content. They also are a form of taking responsibility for the insights that came to us. In the guided image, it must be remembered that no one outside composed it—we ourselves did from some deep level in our being. If we do not understand some image that arises, the key lies within. Often we can get an answer by *asking* the image to tell us what it represents.

2. The Dance of the Selves

Our bodies themselves are often an excellent means of recognizing, integrating and harmonizing our s.p.'s.

In this exercise, stand in a space where (if in a group) you have enough room to have a circle of space as wide as your outstretched arms around you. Close your eyes, and come in contact with your breathing (count ten breaths). With eyes closed, feel yourself in the center of your space and of yourself. Now step out to the edge of your circle and imagine yourself acting out one of your sub-personalities—first an overdeveloped or dominant one. Physically move your body—hands, arms, etc.—in a way that would suit or typify this s.p. Feel yourself totally immersed in this s.p. Then step back to your center, and out of your s.p. Give it a name if possible. Now once again go into your center and come in contact with your breathing. This time step out to the edge of your circle and into a hidden or underdeveloped s.p. that you would like to see become more manifest. Once again develop a physical bodily movement that would express this s.p. After doing so for a few moments, step back into your center, and give it a name. Once again go deeply into your center, using your observed breath as a medium. Now step out to the edge of your circle and assume the bodily movement of the first s.p., and then change into that of the second s.p. Go back and forth between the two. Then try to adopt a bodily motion that would put together both s.p.'s in a way that would harmonize them. Then step back into your center and open your eyes. If alone, write down briefly what happened. If together with others, go around in a circle sharing the name and bodily motion of both the dominant and the dormant s.p.'s.

Finally, use your daily journal to observe, identify and harmonize your s.p.'s as they appear in daily life. More details will be given in our final chapter on journal keeping.

Integration of Body, Mind, Feelings

In addition to the work of the will with sub-personalities, there is another very fruitful area of integration and personal growth. This is through the will and its relationship with body, mind, and feelings. By the body, we mean not only the physical body as such, but the bodily sensations that come to us through what are commonly called the five senses—sight, touch, taste, hearing and smell. It includes the whole realm of bodily movement and expression, such as walking, feeling, touching, dancing, play, sports, work, etc. The sensations are those that directly result from the five senses: e.g., cold, heat, pleasure, fatigue, etc.

The second area is that of the mind or intellect. This is generally the area in which our thoughts, planning and organization take place. Words, ideas and formulas for action come from this center, if we may call it such. By way of distinction, the will can direct the mind to think in a certain area or to develop plans. The will is not simply a part of the mind, but remains over and above it. In our modern technological world the development of the mind can become an all absorbing preoccupation.

The third area is that of the feelings. By these we do not mean the body sensations such as cold, warmth or pain that immediately stem from the body and its sense mechanisms. The feelings we speak of come from a deeper level. We cannot always nicely separate them from bodily sensations, because the two are frequently combined. Examples of such emotions or feelings are those of love, joy, sadness, hatred, anger, jealousy, irritation and others similar. Likewise, these cannot be completely divorced from the mind either. It is thoughts that give rise to many emotions as well as accompany them also.

For progress in personal growth, each of these areas—body, mind and feelings—must develop and grow under the direction of the will. When one area is over-developed, it stifles the others and this hinders the growth of the whole person. For example, in our culture, the most frequent pattern in over-development is that of the mind. Many children start their schooling at the age of five and continue until the end of college, and even into graduate studies. Consequently, as many as twenty or more years are given over essentially to intense cultivation of the mind. Grades, performance in I.Q. tests, state, college and other exams, and qualifications for jobs contribute to high pressure on a person devoted to cultivating the mind. The highest paying professions are usually those associated with the mind: lawyers, doctors, engineers, business, etc. Over-development of the mind leads to a stifling undergrowth of the areas of body and feelings.

In regard to the body area, there are dangers also. This can come about when sports, athletics, work or play is given such time and attention that there is little time or energy for reading, study, and pursuits of the mind. Feelings likewise can suffer, since they need time for their expression and development.

The feelings too can take over and lead to suppression of the mind and body. A person may simply be so overwhelmed by interior feelings and emotions that there is no longer time or energy to devote to the mind or the needs of the body. In fact, when one area, mind, body or feeling, is overstressed to the neglect of the others, the neglected areas eventually refuse to cooperate and may even rebel. For example, the student in college who devotes every possible moment to study may face a rebellion from the body, which will no longer give its needed cooperation to study and may even force a person to give up study and take a needed vacation.

On the other hand, when each of the areas of body, mind, and feelings is given proper attention, they all help one another and the whole person. For example, the student who gives the body proper attention through sports and play actually helps the mind to be more alert and thus study better. Listening to our feelings and becoming more aware of them will make us freer to work with our minds and to use our bodies with less fatigue. When body, mind and feelings are not integrated, we easily tire, and are unable to work steadily for long periods of time. This is because conflict within is draining our energies and preventing us from giving attention to the here and now.

Examples of how body, mind and feelings work together or in opposition will help us understand how we can facilitate a growing harmony of these three areas. First, body and mind. When the body and mind are well coordinated, the body easily accomplishes what the mind has pictured and planned. The trained athlete can imagine throwing a basketball into a hoop. His or her body can then go through the precise motion necessary to do this with great accuracy. The skilled athlete provides an example of a process that goes through all of life. It is important that we learn to walk, move, dance, play and work so that the mind and body work together harmoniously. When the mind is under tension, it is a sign that more attention needs to be given to play, sports, or creative work so that body and mind can reattain their easy harmony.

The second area of integration is between the mind and the feelings. When the mind is over-developed at the expense of the feelings, a process begins to develop that is called rationalization. This means that something is pushed into the mind and dealt with there instead of in the feelings where it belongs. For instance, I may be feeling upset, jealous or angry on the occasion of something a friend or spouse has said or done. This is a feeling and must be dealt with on that level, through awareness and proper expression. Instead, however, I may push it into the mind which begins an endless series of gyrations to discover a reason or excuse that is not on the feeling level. For example, the mind deals with it by saying things like, "We just don't agree on values," or "I was wronged by this person," or "If he or she says this, I will respond this way," etc., etc. It is an endless process because no answers can be found on the mind level. I must be responsible for my feelings and not blame anyone else, or any outward circumstance for them. The outward occasion may be the trigger or occasion for a feeling to come out, but the immediate cause lies within myself. If the process of rationalization grows within us, our minds become tormenting machines that make us live in worry and frustration.

The *third* area is between the feelings and the body. While the feelings have an inner source, they rely on the body for their expression and "discharge" or release. For example, the happy person expresses his or her joy through a facial expression, a smile. On the other hand, a person with a "poker face" has learned to disguise or suppress feelings so that they do not come to the surface. As a result, these feelings clamor for expression and may sometimes bury themselves in an internal organ causing an ulcer or some other inner sickness. It is important then that body and feelings harmonize with one another and help one another.

Exercises, Practices, and Suggestions

1. Congruence and Truth About Our Feelings

In today's highly organized technological age, the greatest difficulty that most people have is the integration of mind and feelings. We are also living in an age of increased physical violence toward others. Crimes of violence toward other persons such as murder, personal injury and rape have been steadily increasing. One cause of this lies in our failure to be deeply aware of feelings and express them honestly to ourselves and others. In contrast, an act of violence results when we substitute a hostile action toward another person for the expression of our feelings. It is literally "taking it out" on someone else instead of the proper bodily expression in ourselves.

The first step is to be aware of our feelings, whether of joy, love, anger, sadness, irritation or worry. The second step is to avoid action if at all possible, while in a state of separating emotions such as anger. This prevents us from hurting or injuring others, or doing things we would later regret. The third step is to have a "muscular discharge" of the emotion. This means to allow it full bodily expression. Really be quiet and feel the emotion that is surging within. Let it permeate the whole body. Stay with the emotion until it dissipates itself. Breathe it deeply in and out until the emotion is fully dissipated. Avoid action meanwhile. The final step is honesty or taking responsibility for our feelings, first to ourselves, and then to others if this is appropriate. Often honesty about our feelings has been misunderstood, and thus has led to increased bitterness with others. An example would be to say to another, "What you said made me very upset." It is correct and honest to say, "I feel very upset and angry." But to say, "*You* made me upset," is to place the blame on another person or outward circumstance. What others say is certainly their own responsibility. Other people are responsible for whatever they say or do, such as insulting remarks or injuries. However, the way we respond to them, with love or hatred, is our own responsibility, not that of others. Otherwise, we would be mere puppets whose feelings are completely under the control of whatever other people might say, do or feel. In the coming chapter on entanglements, we will study ways to get to the root and cause of feelings of anger, irritation, upsetness, and other separating emotions.

2. Anointing, the Biblical Mode of Body and Feeling Integration

The second area of difficulty is the integration of body and feeling. Here we can find valuable help in the biblical practice of anointing.

In his Gospel (7:36–50), Luke tells the story of a woman who came up to Jesus while he was eating in a Pharisee's home and began to wash his feet and anoint them with oil. Simon his host was surprised at this action, not because it was an anointing but because it was done by a strange woman of doubtful reputation. Washing the feet with water and anointing the head with oil were symbols of love and welcome that were customary ways that guests were treated before a banquet. Psalm 23 describes the perfect host in this way, "You anoint my head with oil; my cup overflows" (23:5). During his last visit to Jerusalem, a woman anointed Jesus' head with perfumed oil (Mt 26:6–13). Jesus was immensely pleased with this action and predicted that the story of what she had done would always be told. Jesus also taught his disciples how to cure sick people by anointing them with oil just as he did (Mk 6:12).

This biblical anointing was not the same as a "massage" today. It was not a rubdown, but an expression of love, care and concern. The fingers were used to send the vibrations of love in a person's heart into the body of another through oil which was well known for its penetrating properties. The body, through the fingers and the sense of touch, was able to transmit to other people the deeper feelings of love and concern that lay deep within their hearts.

The following is a meditative and healing exercise that can be done in pairs with a friend, or between parents and children, or with spouses. It can be done on the hands or feet and each person can take a turn in giving or receiving. The pair will sit opposite each other. The receivers will keep their eyes closed, concentrating on their breathing and feelings. The givers will take a little bit of oil and begin to anoint each hand of the other person with gentle strokes and loving care. Do this for five minutes and then reverse roles. This is especially effective for children. The loving hands of their parents have a special healing effect. A good time for this is at bedtime. Since children like to keep their hands active, it is often better to do it on their feet. The oil is not really that necessary. For infants and smaller children, the many times they are handled for washing, changing diapers, etc., can be a much more meaningful experience for both parent and child if a little more time is spent doing this. If time allows, the whole body can be gently stroked.

A final exercise makes use of the powerful inner images that direct and move our lives: Close your eyes and relax, giving attention to your breathing. First concentrate on whatever you hear within the room; then give attention to what you may hear from the outside. Then concentrate on your physical sensations—the feel of the chair or the feeling of your feet on the floor. These are means to arrive at a relaxed, listening state. Now imagine that you are in a favorite meadow. Picture the surroundings as best as you can. Imagine that you see a large treasure chest in the field. Walk over to it and examine it. Now imagine that it is filled with all kinds of treasures and symbols that represent either your mind, your body or your feelings. Open the chest and first find something that represents your body. Do the same for your feelings, and then for your mind. Now enter into dialogue with the symbols. Ask each what it would want from you, and, in turn, tell each what you would want from it. Finally, have them enter into dialogue with one another, exchanging their mutual needs. Now bring them all out into the sun, and watch what takes place in the healing and warming rays of the sun. Next bring them close together, even joining them, and notice in what ways they may blend, harmonize or unite with one another. When you have finished, write down in your notebook the results and conclusions. These may bring you valuable insights as to how to better coordinate your body, feelings and mind.

Some notes on this exercise: Communication deep within us often takes place more through symbols than through words. The guided fantasy we have just made allows us to have much quicker feedback than through dreams. If you do not understand any of the symbols that may arise, just ask them for their meaning and wait for an answer. The sun symbolizes the highest Self, and also the power of the Spirit to transform the faculties of mind, body and feelings so that they can be effective instruments in the loving service of others and the kingdom of God. The dialogue between mind, body and feelings enables us to achieve a better harmony and integration within us by finding out where there is need for development. For example, the body may tell the mind that it will function much better, and think more clearly, if the body has more exercise, fresh air, sports and enjoyment. The will enters into dialogue with each part, in order that mind, body, and feelings may be at the service of the whole person. The will also takes the responsibility of making definite future commitments so that the dialogue between the faculties will bear fruit. The final blending of the faculties under the sun is quite a natural process because body, mind, and feelings are not really distinct and separate but flow into one another. The images themselves may change under the transforming influence of the sun.

Points for group or class discussion or personal reference:

1. Name both a dominant and a recessive (hidden) sub-personality that you have discovered. Introduce them to yourself or to others. How can you help each one of these to have its proper contribution to your personal development? How can each of them serve you better?

2. In reference to mind, body and feelings: share the name or symbol you have found for each. Describe the dialogue that took place between them in the exercise. What directions for the future did this give you?

Annotated Bibliography For Further Reading

Assagioli, R., *The Act of the Will* (N.Y.: Viking, 1973). A book describing practical ways to strengthen the will and use it skillfully in the personal growth process.

Ferrucci, P., *What We May Be* (Los Angeles: J.P. Tarcher, 1982). Ferrucci, a successor of Assagioli, provides a goldmine of imagery exercises and meditative approaches to help develop the use of the will in personal integration.

7

Overcoming Entanglements
and Roadblocks

In questionnaires, people have often been asked what they want most from life. The more frequent answer is "happiness." Experience however teaches us that the search for happiness is a very elusive one. Happiness often comes when we least expect it and even as the result of forgetfulness of self or through suffering.

The root meaning of the word "happiness" can give us a clue as to why the search can be so elusive, and sometimes unproductive. The word "happiness" in English comes from the root "hap," meaning a chance of some kind. Thus we get the words "to happen" or a "happening." A *hapless* person is one without luck. A "happy-go-lucky" individual drifts here and there without concern, depending on luck. "Haphazard" and "mishaps" also come from this root. For most people happiness indeed does depend on whether or not some outside person, thing or event comes to pass that will satisfy some desire they already have in their mind or imagination. Consequently, happiness depends on external matters rather than what they have inside of them. But are not desires a part and fabric of life itself? Could we possibly have "happiness" without satisfaction of our desires?

It all depends on whether we just have desires or whether desires have us. When they have a hold on us and cause us suffering when we do not attain them, then they may be called "hang-ups" or "addictions"—outside things we feel we must have in order to be happy. When these desires are simply preferences, causing no suffering when we are deprived of them, then they can bring us unexpected extra joy when they are fulfilled. An example can easily bring out the difference between an entangling addiction and a preference. If I have a preference for either drinking or smoking, then if my cigarette or bottle is lost or taken away,

I maintain my inner peace and happiness. If I become more than momentarily angry, upset or irritated, then it is an addiction, hang-up or entanglement, not just a simple desire or attachment.

What difference does this make in day-to-day living? When no effort is made to overcome addictions, we lead a merry-go-round type of existence with "good days" and "bad days," highs or lows depending on whether our entangling desire for something outside is fulfilled. Yet, unfortunately, even fulfillment often gives only momentary peace because an even greater desire is created by giving in to the addiction. More demands result so that the graph of "highs and lows" begins to look like this: the level of the "high" becomes lower and lower while the level of the "lows" with all its depression keeps going down. We become "object" centered instead of person oriented. We want certain people because they satisfy certain demands or expectations such as power or sex; otherwise we find little "use" for them. Everything becomes centered about outside things in proportion to their ability to satisfy inner models, desires or expectations.

When our life is governed by such addictions, we lead a fragile, enslaved life. We walk around, as it were, clothed by outside balloons. Life becomes fragile because we may not be able to satisfy our heavy attachment in some particular circumstance and thus a balloon is broken. Other people, too, notice our insecurity and sometimes take delight in poking needles in our balloons to expose our weakness. We lead a dependent life, a fearful life, never knowing when our happiness can be either found or lost in a moment.

This is why Jesus made such strong statements about eradicating such addictions. In regard to money, for example, he said: "No one can serve two masters; for either he will hate the one and love the other, or he will be devoted to the one and despise the other. You cannot serve God and mammon" (Mt 6:24). About the addiction to sex he said:

> You have heard that it was said "You shall not commit adultery," But I say to you that everyone who looks at a woman lustfully has already committed adultery with her in his heart (Mt 5:27–28).

Centuries before Jesus, Buddha formulated his noble truths outlining the path to illumination and happiness. The first truth is the recognition and awareness of the painful reality of suffering in the world. The second truth is the realization that most of this suffering is caused by ourselves, by letting our desires get out of hand. The third truth is that we must search for and eradicate the desires that are at the root of our unhappiness.

The remedy then is rather simple and can be phrased in this way: We must change our addictions into simple preferences. Let us take an example of the difference between an addiction and a preference in regard to sex. Suppose or imagine I spend a day with someone who is very dear to me. If sex is a preference, I enjoy his or her company, conversation and the things we do together. If it so happens that sex is impossible, or that he or she does not wish it on that day, that is O.K. I am at peace and happy with our time together. If we do have sex, it is like extra cream on a cake that is beautiful and delicious as it is. It is a deeply fulfilling personal union. I have enjoyed every moment of our company. If, however, I am addicted to sex, this is always on my mind. The image of being together in bed dominates so that I cannot give proper attention to the here-and-now of the beautiful things we can share and do together. If I do not have sex, I feel frustrated and feel that the day has been lost. If I do have sex, chances are that because my mind has been continuously focusing on the future, the beauties of those moments may be largely lost also and that the relationship will be more on an object level than a deep personal union.

So if we want to seriously move on the path of personal growth, we must make serious efforts to change our addictions into preferences. The first step is to recognize and be aware of our addictions. This is not hard to do. All that is necessary is to be aware of separating emotions in daily life (that separate us from others)—anger, frustration, boredom, jealousy, etc. I do not mean fleeting feelings, but those that hang on. Then we must pinpoint the cause of this in the form of the demand, model or expectation in our mind that we are placing on this person or situation. Next we take full responsibility for this in this form: I am making myself (angry, upset, etc.) because I am addictively demanding that.

The next step is to effectively deal with this emotional mind program that has built up, perhaps over the years. We must fully experience the suffering it has caused us and be totally determined to remove the addiction and change it into a preference.

Two Exercises in Changing Addictions into Preferences

1. A situation in which you have been upset through an addiction can be healed and transformed into an opportunity of growth. When you are in a quiet loving space, imagine in your mind the last situation in which you experienced a separating emotion. Go into the feelings you had at the time and stay with them. Let your whole body enter into them. When you have passed through this and you are in a calm, loving place once more, look at the whole situation through a filter of forgiveness, love and acceptance. Imagine yourself speaking, acting and responding from this loving place. Once you have done this, you have brought a powerful healing influence into your life as the whole situation has now helped you to grow by an important step in lessening the power of addictions over you or removing them completely.

2. Formulate a strong emotion-backed phrase that directly contradicts your addiction, e.g., ''I don't have to take alcohol or drugs to be happy,'' or ''I don't have to have a neat tidy room or house.'' The following is a little secret to help ''reprogram'' through such phrases: The area of the head and brain around the ear is most delicate and sensitive. Take your right hand and with your fingers keep tracing a circle around your ear following the bone ridge in your skull. Do it with a counter-clockwise motion, repeating the reprogramming phrases above. The right ear is more associated with the negative orders or structural part of the brain. Next take your left hand and make the same motion around your left ear. This time use a positive phrase instead, e.g., ''I love and accept you as you are,'' or some phrase relative to the specific situation. This is a positive affirmation better associated with the left or more positive and receptive side. The positive statement is really one of unconditional love—what is most needed. Do the motion ten or more times on each side, repeating the phrases with determination and feeling.

What should we do if we find ourselves engulfed by a strong separating emotion such as anger or jealousy? First of all, *don't act* in such a state because you will almost certainly hurt yourself or others. Of course, if the house is burning down, by all means act and get out quickly! The second step is to deliberately experience our emotion fully by ''muscular discharge.'' This means letting the feeling slowly diffuse through our whole body. A good way to do this is through deliberately breathing the emotion in and out. For example, ''anger in'' on the in-breath, and "anger out" on the out-breath. Or we can truthfully admit verbally, "Right now I am feeling a lot of (e.g.) anger." In itself this is a helpful release. If we apply the breathing technique, we can breathe in and out in the way described until we feel at peace once again. If circumstances do not allow sufficient time, at least do this for a few breaths and come back to it again later in the day.

It is remarkable that most people will give us "space" if we honestly admit our feelings. The natural tendency is to "escape" in some way either by diversion, alcohol, drugs or in some other way so the uptight feeling goes away. We are drawn to the "quick way." However, giving in to this tendency means that a separating emotion is temporarily repressed or buried and thus gains more power over us by lodging itself inside our bodily organs.

Entanglements and Personal Relationships

One of the best ways to steadily grow during life is through meaningful personal relationships. At the same time, there are few things in life that cost us more sadness, grief and heaviness of heart than the breakup of a relationship. The memories of moments of beautiful openness together with generosity and sacrifice as well as deeply shared emotions stay with us and often cause more additional sorrow. All we have to do is pick up the daily paper where the divorce announcements often outnumber the marriages. And then of course there are so many marriages where people stay together in a kind of "cease-fire" arrangement with little real love or joy. What is the cause of most of these separations? Most people, if questioned, would be ready with answers. They quickly blame the other person—their character, temperament, habits, lifestyle—you name it.

And yet what is often the *real cause*? The real cause lies within themselves and not the other person. We have seen that when we experience separating emotions such as anger, boredom, jealousy, and bitterness, it is due to the *demands* and *expectations* in our own *minds* that we have placed on another person. When they do not conform to this model, then we become upset in some way. The habit of criticizing, blaming and judging other people comes from the desire to force everyone into the mental mold or model we have of others.

What are we to do if we find ourselves in a relationship and wish to personally grow together? The first step is to take responsibility for our own separating emotions by finding the addictions that cause them (see our method described previously). The second accompanying step is to stop blaming or criticizing our partner as the source of our unhappiness. The third step will take a great burden off our friend or spouse. This is to honestly admit to them the addictions that are at the source of our unhappiness. For example, instead of saying, "I am upset and angry because your clothes and things are all over the house," I can say, "I am *making myself* upset because I am demanding that the house be kept in order." This does not mean that I cannot prefer orderliness and manifest this preference to another person. The difference is this: when a preference is not fulfilled, I remain peaceful and happy. If it is a demand, I become upset and angry.

Once we start to do this, a beautiful openness and honesty takes the place of hiding our weaknesses and criticizing others. We can become partners in growth during the great adventure of life instead of obstacles to one another. More important yet, we will gradually reach to true unconditioned love of others. This is a love that remains constant and true *no matter what the other person says or does*. If it is a love based on certain conditions—that a person act in accord with my model—then it is not true love; it is conditional, based not on the person as he or she is, but only on the *condition* that he or she fulfills my mental models.

A final very effective exercise is to repeat each day a beautiful summary for obtaining true peace and happiness called the Twelve Pathways. These are from the best seller book by Ken Keyes, Jr., called *Handbook to Higher Consciousness* which can be found in most bookstores. The Twelve Pathways are here quoted by permission of the publisher. I am indebted also to Ken for many personal insights in this book. The following are the Twelve Pathways to the Higher Consciousness Planes of Unconditional Love and Oneness:

1. I am freeing myself from security, sensation, and power addictions that make me try to forcefully control situations in my life, and thus destroy my serenity and keep me from loving myself and others.

2. I am discovering how my consciousness-dominating addictions create my illusory version of the changing world of people and situations around me.

3. I welcome the opportunity (even if painful) that my minute to min-

ute experience offers me to become aware of the addictions I must reprogram to be liberated from my robot-like emotional patterns.

4. I always remember that I have everything I need to enjoy my here and now unless I am letting my consciousness be dominated by demands and expectations based on the dead past or the imagined future.

5. I take full responsibility here and now for everything I experience, for it is my own programming that creates my actions and also influences the reactions of people around me.

6. I accept myself completely here and now and consciously experience everything I feel, think, say, and do (including my emotion-backed addictions) as a necessary part of my growth into higher consciousness.

7. I open myself genuinely to all people by being willing to fully communicate my deepest feelings since hiding in any degree keeps me stuck in my illusion of separateness from other people.

8. I feel with loving compassion the problems of others without getting caught up emotionally in their predicaments that are offering them messages they need for their growth.

9. I act freely when I am tuned in, centered, and loving, but if possible I avoid acting when I am emotionally upset and depriving myself of the wisdom that flows from love and expanded consciousness.

10. I am continually calming the restless scanning of my rational mind in order to perceive the finer energies that enable me to unitively merge with everything around me.

11. I am constantly aware of which of the Seven Centers of Consciousness (cf. Chapter 1) I am using, and I feel my energy, perceptiveness, love and inner peace growth as I open all of the Centers of Consciousness.

12. I am perceiving everyone, including myself, as an awakening being who is here to claim his or her birthright to the higher consciousness planes of unconditional love and oneness.

Points for group or class discussion as well as individual reflection:

1. What popular misunderstandings of happiness are used by TV commercials to sell their products? Give some examples.

2. What is the difference between an addiction and a simple preference? Illustrate with some examples. Contrast the difference in results when a person obtains or loses a preference or a craving.

3. What is the real test to discover whether we really have an addiction? Think of some examples or personal experiences.

4. What are some good ways to turn addictions into preferences and thus open the way to a happier life? Recall some occasions when you or others have done this.

Annotated Bibliography for Further Reading

Keyes, Ken, Jr., *Handbook For Higher Consciousness* (Coos Bay, Or.: Vision, 1975). Millions of people young and old have read this book and found it most valuable in overcoming the roadblocks and addictions that impede our happiness and personal growth.

Trungpa, C., *Cutting Through Spiritual Materialism* (Berkeley: Shambala, 1973). A well known eastern master points out deceptive pitfalls to personal growth in a series of conferences.

8

The Sacrament of Each Moment

The keynote of Jesus' whole career and preaching was, "The kingdom of God is at hand." Most people then as now looked to the future for the important times in life—graduation, vacations, promotions, retirement, etc. In Jesus' time, many people expected a great future intervention of God that would bring peace and justice to the earth and set the world right. Others lived in the past, remembering God's great work in past history, limiting his action to what he had done in the past and continually recalling them in ritual observances and laws. Jesus' message was revolutionary: You have all you need right here and now, through God's presence and power. No need to look to the distant imaginary future or the dead past. When people asked him about signs that would indicate the future coming of God, Jesus pointed to the supreme present reality by saying, "The kingdom of God is in your midst" (Lk 17:21).

Jesus did not merely limit himself to proclaiming the present reality of the kingdom. He specifically warned about the danger of preoccupation about the future. He said in the Sermon on the Mount, "Do not worry about tomorrow, for tomorrow will have anxieties of its own" (Mt 6:34). He went into detail about the matter of worry, for it is essentially a preoccupation of the mind about the future. He said:

> Therefore I tell you, do not be anxious about your life, what you shall eat or what you shall drink, nor about your body, what you shall put on. Is not life more than food, and the body more than clothing? Look at the birds of the air: they neither sow nor reap nor gather into barns, and yet your heavenly Father feeds them. Are you not of more value than they? (Mt. 6:25–26).

God's Work in the Universe

The ultimate truth behind the here and now way of living is that God is working in the universe and that each of us plays an important part in that work. Thus every event in life has an important meaning for us. Every person we meet is a special teacher with an important message for us. All of nature is a shining path leading to God.

Most people find it hard to accept a God who is controlling the events of the world, somewhat as the director of a puppet show pulls all the strings. This view of God is an unacceptable mechanistic view that would force us to blame God for all the evil and violence in the world. How could we say that the murder of six million Jews by Hitler and his cohorts during World War II is part of the providence of God? Could we believe that the murder of an innocent bystander by a drunken driver is a part of God's eternal plan?

Instead we must admit that we ourselves bear responsibility for evil and violence by the abuse of the God-given freedom we possess. God has placed his power within the universe and especially in human beings. The world is in God and God is in the world. In a sense, God has deliberately renounced power by a supreme act of love in "letting go" and placing all his power in all of the universe. Leaving us free means that freedom of choice can be abused. We can live, if we choose, on the level of personal security, pleasure and power. This results in suffering and sometimes even death to others when they happen to stand in our way.

What then does the "providence of God" mean? God has renounced power and his role as protector, controller and policeman so that, through his presence in each person and in the whole universe, he can treat us as an equal and we can have him as a supreme Friend. It is characteristic of a friend that he or she does not provide answers for our problems, but rather is an *answering person*—one who answers for us or stands by us when it really counts. Having a friend does not mean an escape from sickness, suffering, accidents, or anything that might happen to any other person. It does mean that we have a special and unique resource that another may not realize is present. Actually, the greater the suffering or misfortune that comes to us, the more our friend is present to us in love and understanding. Thus even a tragic loss can be the occasion of a new and special outpouring of the friend's love.

The same is true of God. God lets events move in a mysterious way.

Some things appear completely unexplainable and ridiculous: the premature accidental death of a child, a long painful terminal cancer, a freak automobile accident immobilizing a person for life. Yet God the friend is present to and in each one of us. Every wound becomes the occasion of special healing love that leaves us actually stronger than before. There is a new energy that goes with every event of life—an energy in proportion to the need of the occasion. We can say, then, that there is a *sacrament of each moment* as the external occasion becomes the clear vessel for God's love and presence to shine through.

Some Elements and Suggestions About Living Here and Now

1. The unplanned, unforeseen events of life are often the most fruitful. As I am writing this, someone interrupted me to ask, "What are you writing about?" I "lose time" to explain all about it to her. But actually I have not *lost time* but gained time by trying to be open to the new and unknown. The *interruptions* of life are very special opportunities. When we are *interrupted,* God's energy *erupts* and bursts forth into the world. Whatever is spontaneous and uncontrolled has great possibilities for the presence of God to manifest itself. In the case of my own "interruption" I was rewarded by a beautiful moment of sharing truth and an understanding, loving smile. The fact that my own mental plans are disrupted forces me into a new openness to the world around me. I begin to experience the world as it is, rather than in accord with the constructs in my mind.

New Energy and Vitality

2. Strain, stress and anxiety are all by-products of our modern technological age. Fatigue and tiredness are often caused by the energy drain that results from fighting reality and the situations of life rather than flowing with them. We all move along the stream of life with many other drops of water like ourselves. If we build useless dams along the way, we only waste precious energy without necessity. When our minds are preoccupied with the past or present, an effective block or dam is set up that keeps up from experiencing the life-giving and energizing forces in the people and world around us. When we live in the here and now, we

will no longer be drained by our work or occupation. Instead we will find fresh energy in every new situation.

Avoid Hurry

3. Haste makes waste—similar proverbs are found in many languages. Haste and hurry are prompted by the desire to get something done or accomplished. It is essentially preoccupation with the future. A deliberately slower pace will make us more alive, aware and energetic as we learn to experience the fullness of each moment. Slowing down can help us enjoy the process of life rather than looking to various end products. Try walking slower, talking slower—let your body move more calmly and reflectively. Most Americans fret and grit their teeth when faced by unplanned delays such as even a traffic light or waiting in line. Look upon an unexpected wait as an opportunity to stop and just *be* instead of always *doing* something. It can also be a time to practice your favorite mantras (cf. Chapter 9).

Totality

4. Whatever we do half-heartedly is literally as well as figuratively "a drag." If we do not give full attention, some part of our being is resisting or fighting the real here and now, instead of lovingly accepting it. I use the word *acceptance* rather than *resignation*. Resignation implies a passive "giving-in" which is also a loss of energy, since it does not allow us to use our innate energies. Paul, in writing to the Colossians, understood the Christian commitment in the sense of a beautiful totality in whatever we think, say or do. He wrote:

> Whatever your work is, put your heart into it as if it were for the Lord (3:23).

We have all observed how beautiful it is when someone listens to us totally or gives us complete attention. It seems to draw the very best from the depths of our heart. So it is when we give total attention to our work, to people and to the events of daily life. We begin to draw new invigorating energies from what others might consider as ordinary or even "boring."

Payoffs Waste Energy

5. Throughout life many actions are motivated by some kind of payoff—a reward, a salary or some kind of material gain. Students often study motivated by the prestige and benefits of high marks. Men and women plod through their work, looking forward to raises, promotions or retirement benefits. All of this means that attention is directed not to the work or study but to something outside of it. This results in a serious loss of energy as resistance is built up to work or study that gives no pleasure or joy in itself but only as a tool for some other benefit. The only remedy is to keep asking ourselves, "Would I be willing to work at this job or occupation if there were no money or profit from it?" If not, I am not living in the here and now.

Exercises

An exercise for living here and now could be a trap—we could actually miss the message of the here and now by substituting an exercise for it. There is really no gimmick to make us give attention to the present moment. However, if we find difficulty in concentration because of our wandering minds, the following will be helpful.

First of all, in general:

1. Review what we have written on the breath and meditation. Variations of this can be used to help concentration: Count your breaths in and out until you reach fifteen. Listen to your heartbeat. Place your breath in synchrony with your heartbeat. When we concentrate on our breath and heart, we are in touch with the core of our life—it will be impossible for the mind to be elsewhere.

2. When you find yourself imprisoned by distractions that keep you from present awareness, ask yourself two questions like this: "Where are you, Joseph Grassi?" (Here!) "What time is it, Joseph Grassi?" (Now!)

3. The mania for "doing things"—projects designed by the mind—can keep us from quietly *being* with the reality of each moment.

More specifically the following exercises can be helpful:
This first exercise deals with one of the great obstacles to living here

and now: dwelling excessively on the past. Yet we must first realize why we do this to such an extent that we often lose out on the beautiful here and now, thus causing the joys of life to pass us by. It is useless to merely try, by force of will, not to think of the past. Either we will repress it, which will be harmful, or we will only increase its power over us. If we go back to the past so often, it is because something inside is telling us that we should. In other words, there is something unresolved back in the past that must be taken care of. If we do not do this, we will go back again and again in frustration until this is done.

What types of unresolved matters does the past hold that need to be examined and resolved, as well as healed? These may be events we have not accepted, relationships still holding bitterness, or wounds we have received from others or given to them. What can actually be done about these past matters? It is possible to relive these occasions or relationships and heal them at their roots. This is because all these matters have left images with us that are very present and real. Fortunately we can change them.

A good way to do this is to imagine an event or occasion in the past that really upset us. Go through the whole event, dialogue or happening. Hear again what was being said or done. Go into the feelings you had on this occasion, and fully experience them, whether they were sorrow, anger or any other emotion. Take ample time to do this. Now go back to the incident's beginning, and approach it with a feeling of acceptance of yourself, and other people. Feel now a real concern and love for the people involved in the incident. Now recreate a whole new event with them that goes along with your new feelings. What you are doing is creating a new image or tape that heals the past so it is no longer fearful, but an occasion of happiness and forgiveness. This is the result of what Jesus refers to as "forgiving from the heart" (Mt 18:35).

The following areas will need to be explored and healed by this exercise, which can be called "healing memories"—relationships with parents, even if they are dead and many years have passed. We need to first accept and love our parents unconditionally if we are to move fast in the path of personal growth. Then we can move into other relationships—broken friendships or incidents where we have been hurt by another, or where we have hurt someone else. We cannot move rapidly into happiness with a heavy heart about the past, or a wound within that has never been healed. This exercise can be done alone, with someone else, or in a small supporting group.

A second exercise goes to another obstacle to living in the beautiful here-and-now. Our daily activities very quickly become automated, so we can do them with minimal attention. We can be walking through a forest on a beautiful summer day and not even advert to our walking and all the beauty around us. Or we can drive along a scenic highway barely noticing the wonders of nature around us. Somehow our controls have been placed on ''automatic.''

A very fruitful practice is to take a walk and deliberately not dwell our minds on anything except what we actually see, hear, feel or smell. If thoughts do come to the mind, we will just take note of them and return to concentration on the immediate perceptions of our senses. In this way, a whole new world—the world as it is—can become open to us, instead of the old inner world of our images, models, plans, and expectations of how the world should be. The same exercise can be used while driving or doing other things. It is amazing that even while driving, if we give real attention to the motor, the car, the highway, the people in other cars, we will be driving much better, and the experience will become alive and exciting.

A third exercise concerns the future. What causes us to dwell in the future, in a world that may never be, and not give attention to the ''sacrament of each moment''? One reason lies in the built-up mental world of expectations of what we want in the way of security, money, prestige, pleasure and power. Consequently, we imagine all those things that will give us that artificial world. The only real cure for this is a new direction of life built on Jesus' advice: ''Seek first his kingdom, his righteousness, and all these things shall be yours as well'' (Mt 6:33). What is this kingdom? Paul describes it as follows: ''The kingdom of God does not mean food and drink, but righteousness and peace and joy of the Holy Spirit'' (Rom 14:17).

So when we find ourselves dwelling excessively on the future, or occupied with worries, the best approach is to regard this as a challenge, an opportunity, a chance for decision—or even a temptation. We can ask ourselves, ''How does this bring about the kingdom of God, with its justice, peace and joy of the Holy Spirit?'' or ''What are my priorities in life?'' It can be the occasion of repeating the short petition from the

Lord's Prayer, "Thy kingdom come," or some other petition such as "Lead us not into temptation." Once we have done this, then we can turn back gently to the occupation of the moment. The future will no longer have power over us if we look forward with hope and trust to the future, knowing that God will give us not necessarily all we want, but all that we really need to make possible his kingdom of justice, peace and joy.

Finally, and this may be the most insidious obstacle: we may find it difficult to live in the present because, even unknowingly, we may not be giving attention to feelings of our body, e.g., pain or tiredness or inner feelings such as anger, boredom, irritation or jealousy. These may be clamoring for our attention. Consequently we may give ourselves only partially to the person or event at the moment. These signals are telling us to STOP as soon as we can.

Inner feelings such as anger need to be acknowledged and experienced; otherwise they will erupt like a volcano in violent action. The following approach can be very helpful: breathe deeply in and out the inner feeling, e.g., anger-in, anger-out, until you can totally experience it. Continue until you feel peaceful and calm. Then get at the roots and cause as in Chapter 6. The same can be done with pain. If we fight against tiredness, we only consume more energy in a losing battle. True living here and now may mean more rest and sleep!

Points for group or class discussion as well as individual reflection:

1. What is the basic meaning of the "Sacrament of Each Moment"? How is this connected to the message of Jesus?

2. How can the future or the past help us toward an appreciative awareness of the here and now? How can they impede it? How can we effectively deal with upsetting past events or troublesome future possibilities?

3. From your experience as well as from the text, what practical suggestions would you have that would help toward living each moment fully?

Annotated Bibliography For Further Study

Killinger, J., *The Cup and the Waterfall: The Adventure of Living in the Present Moment* (Ramsey, N.J.: Paulist, 1983). The author's inspirational view is that God's presence inundates our whole life if we learn to cultivate a deep receptivity to his grace.

Ram Dass, *The Only Dance There Is* (Garden City, N.Y.: Doubleday, 1974). A former professor at Harvard describes his journey away from drugs and psychedelics to find enlightenment in the dance of life, the here and now.

9

Pain and Death:
The Neglected Road to Life

Meditation is nothing more than a deep awareness of who we really are. At our roots is the breath of life, the Holy Spirit. Yet death is as much a part of us as life. A new-born baby taking its first breath begins living outside the womb, but also begins the process of dying. Death does not merely lie in the future. It is a process continually at work in every cell of the body. Consequently, it is supremely important to be aware of death and its meaning. Unnecessary resistance to the death process can be a serious obstacle to personal growth.

However, is it not depressing to dwell on death? On the very contrary, death is actually the key to life. Death does not mean non-existence, but a movement from one type of existence to another. Both are sustained by the powerful Spirit of God. Before a child is born, it must "die." When the umbilical cord is severed, the dependent life on its mother's nourishing blood ends so that a new type of life may begin. In fact, all of life is made possible by death. Dead leaves from trees and decaying animals enable the soil to obtain the organic matter necessary for plants to grow. When our own bodies die, a new dimension of existence begins that is supported by the Spirit of God. Saint Paul calls this a "pneumatic" (Greek) or spirit-transformed body in contrast to our present natural or physical bodies (1 Cor 15:44).

Awareness of Death: The Pathway to a
More Vibrant Life—Some Hints

1. *Welcome the signs of death.* The internal process of death manifests itself through many external signs. Some are quite small and easily overlooked. It may be a cut or a bruise, a common cold, a short illness,

a fall, a toothache, a headache or some kind of pain. Other signs are more striking and make us feel the shadow of death around us. This may be the death of a close friend or relative, a serious illness, an accident with a narrow escape from death, a serious injury or handicap, or even old age. Each of these illustrates some way that death is part of our being, a process that will come to completion either in the far future or at some near unexpected moment.

To welcome the signs of death means to accept the death process many times so that when it comes to completion, we will be fully prepared and ready. When we do so, we conquer the greatest fear of all—that of losing our lives. This fear consumes a major part of our energies—energies that could be used to promote vibrant growth. Instead of fighting the inevitable—*what actually is*—we can flow along with it and strengthen the life process in doing so. The objection remains, "If we give in to sickness and weakness, would this not hurt our health? Is not the 'will to live' supremely important?"

To welcome death's signs does not mean that we put aside the desire for healing and better health. In fact, we promote the healing process by conquering the fear that paralyzes growth and healing. The signs of death are always present. It is a useless drain of energy to fight them. By welcoming them instead of resisting them, we can give better attention to life and the healing process that is also going on.

2. *Take advantage of the STOP signs.* The road of life has an ultimate, supreme STOP sign which is death. Yet life contains innumerable smaller STOP signs on its many streets that force us to stop and then go again. Just above we have enumerated some of these: pain, sickness, accidents, etc. If we observe most people in the world around us, we find that the last thing they want to do is to be forced to stop. We have all had the experience of driving a car at the speed limit and watching most cars speeding by us—some at very high speeds. Most people are hurrying to get somewhere or even nowhere. No one really wants to stop. Yet something inside of them really does want to stop so they outwardly go faster and faster until something really does stop them. There is really an inner cause for many accidents resulting from speed.

An important secret of personal growth is to make use of the many STOP signs we face in daily life. We have just discussed some of the major ones. But life is filled with smaller STOP signs that we often drive through, making ourselves more vulnerable to loss. Recently, there was a garage sale on the block near my house. This is usually a quiet street. The residents drive slowly along it and watch the other quiet streets for cars. However, this weekend attracted many cars from other areas— some people rushing from one garage sale to another to snatch the best buys as early as possible. Consequently, there were two serious accidents on just one weekend at a very quiet intersection that had no STOP sign. Next week there was a traffic meter on the road to ascertain if the traffic warranted the installation of a STOP sign that would force people to stop.

The small STOP signs of daily life are so ordinary that we hardly give attention to them—except by way of frustration. Examples are waiting for a traffic light, waiting for other people at home or in a store, the "loss" of time caused by a breakdown of machinery, appliances, etc. The list could be almost endless—we could even include the coffee breaks, the bathroom stops, etc. All of these can be great opportunities, rather than occasions of frustration and irritation, if we only welcome them and make use of them for quiet moments of awareness and meditation, or for attention to our breathing and inner feelings.

The above stops are all involuntary. We must make them anyway, so why not welcome them? This is hard with our American mania for doing things. That is why it is a great help to have some *voluntary stops* each day. These can be sometimes long, where we practice the Zen type of meditation already described. When we quiet down or stop the body, then the mind and emotions gradually quiet down so we can go deeper within. The voluntary stops can also be short such as a definite "break" in the afternoon, morning or evening. This could be as brief as a few moments. When we take voluntary stops, we will be better prepared for the involuntary stops that life brings us. The planned little stops make us ready for the unexpected stops and the supreme unplanned stop, death itself.

3. *Tapping New Powers, or How Never To Forget.* Imagine the fourth quarter of an exciting ball game. The score is tied, and there are only two minutes left to play. We can sense something unusual happening to both players and audience. There seems to be a spell over everyone resulting in complete attention and absorption in what is going on. A burst of new energy and awareness comes over the players. Extraordi-

nary things often happen toward the end of a ball game. The last two minutes seem longer than the entire first part of the game. Time appears to stretch out and almost stop.

What causes this phenomenon? Every game is really an image of life itself. Life has a fixed amount of time for its "game," just as a sporting competition. The plays and final score are irreversible. In parallel, there is a sense of uniqueness and ultimacy in life. At times we experience this in an overpowering way. It may be the last words of a parent or friend, a last embrace, a last conversation. There is a very precious quality about these moments, because all of life is summed up in them. At these times, as in our ball game illustration, we become supremely aware; new energy bursts out, and time becomes almost eternal as the clock slows down.

The secret of tapping new powers and bringing the eternal into each moment is to recover the ultimacy of life in the "ordinary" events of each day. "Ordinary" is in quotation marks, because there are really no merely ordinary moments of each day. There is a uniqueness and once-and-for-all quality in even a "chance" conversation that will never be repeated, not for all eternity. All we need to do is to recover this sense of ultimacy, for example when someone is speaking to us. If we do so, we will experience a mysterious power in our words and theirs. We will soon arrive at a deep interpersonal communion that is beyond words.

This will all happen when you let your mind go. There is simply *no time* for figuring out the cost, how long the conversation will last, what else you might be doing, etc. You are just listening to *last words* that are unique, and unrepeatable. But will we not be drained by giving such attention to people and events? Will they not devour all of our time? To the contrary, you will discover new energies both for yourself and for them. You will find that you actually accomplish more and in less time. Many people spend so much time talking because they feel they are not being listened to. So they try again and again. When we *listen* deeply to persons and events, satisfaction and peace soon comes because we are no longer watching the clock.

How does this answer the question "how never to forget"? A last moment is never forgotten because of the complete awareness we have given to that moment. We often lose things or forget because we have become innerly "lost" by worry or preoccupation keeping us from awareness of each moment. When a sense of ultimacy is recovered, we make fewer mistakes, lose fewer articles, and rarely forget what is said or done. When we do lose articles, or forget, it is a warning to go within and recover our awareness of the present and even eternal moments of life.

Death is the supreme breaker of every routine. It is the unplanned, the unexpected. Few people plan their own deaths. Even if they plan some of the externals, they can never chart their own reactions to their oncoming death. If we deliberately break routines during life, we will not have to await death. We will have already died by experiencing the psychological effects of death.

Death Is Our Best Counselor

Death is not a mysterious dark stranger—an enemy who comes to take away our precious life. Death is part of our very being. It is not impersonal, but truly part of our person. So we should really call death our friend—our very dear friend. A friend is one who can help us in time of crisis or need. Today, the counseling professions continue to grow as more and more people turn to professional help to face the increasing pressures of our modern world. These counselors play a very important part in modern life. Yet most of the good they accomplish is by helping people develop their own resources.

Often, the trip to the therapist symbolizes and accompanies an inner journey where the real healing process takes place. When we take the journey within, we will never receive anything but the best advice. We will never be led astray. Since death is our inner friend, death is also our best counselor. When we call upon death for advice, or when we consider life's situations in view of death, we will always receive the very best counsel. All it takes is a minute or two. Just formulate your question and ask death for advice. You will often be surprised by the answers that come, and you will not make a mistake in following them.

A Meditation and Guided Fantasy— To Be Repeated From Time to Time

(Begin after breathing and relaxing exercises as already described.)
Imagine you are visiting your doctor because of some health problem. You receive a very careful physical examination, take numerous

tests, and make an appointment to come back for a consultation. When you return, the physician appears very concerned, though kind and understanding. The doctor takes you by the hand and says, "I am sorry, but all the tests and examinations show you have a serious illness. I can help ease the pain but not cure you." Alarmed, you ask, "Tell me the truth, doctor, how long do I have to live?" The doctor answers, "About six months."

Shocked by this, you go off by yourself and consider the implications of this sudden turn in your life. (Give yourself time to do this, and other parts of the fantasy.) See yourself at first angry, frustrated, and then gradually coming to terms with your approaching death. Then decide who, if anyone, you are going to tell about this. See yourself telling them, and observe their reactions. Then make plans for what you want to do during these months. Finally the time comes when you have only a few weeks to live. Imagine this and the pain that may be present, physically and emotionally. Finally, there are only a few days. In your imagination, live these last days and hours with your loved ones. Imagine what you will want to say to them, and they to you. Finally you are in the last hour, the last few moments. Imagine yourself breathing the last ten breaths of your life—actually breathe and count them.

What you have done in this fantasy is not pure imagination but a shortening and capsulizing of all life. We are all "terminally ill" since no one can escape death. In this exercise, we have merely put it all together in six months—which we may not have at all! It is important *always* to live as if you had at the most six months to go, and to experience in life all you would want to do during these six months. This practice can be united to that of strengthening the will in Chapter 5. In our journals (cf. the last chapter) we can note what we will do tomorrow, next week, next month, the next six months, according to the instructions of the "I can't, I won't, I'll try" exercise in Chapter 5. All this can be best accomplished in light of the death meditation.

Practice—To Be Repeated Once a Year

Go to a funeral home and make arrangements for a death—your own. Why leave other people with the burden of this, especially since they may not make arrangements in accord with your own wishes? Talk everything over with the funeral director. Among other things the following should be discussed: type of services, the cost. How do you want your body cared for: embalmed, buried, cremated? If buried, where and how? If cremated, what about the ashes? Buried? Given in a jar to your relatives? Scattered at sea? etc. Would you give permission for parts of your body to be donated to others, e.g., a heart transplant? How do you arrange for this legally? All the above should be in writing so those nearest to you will have a precise idea of what you want for your funeral. However, do not be rigid in your directions. The funeral service is more for them than it is for you.

Practice—To Be Reviewed Every Six Months

With the help of a good lawyer draw up your will. Give the lawyer also a copy of your financial assets: names of banks, number of accounts, place of safe deposit boxes, other valuables. List the address of properties or houses you may own. Other assets such as stocks, bonds, automobiles, etc., should be listed along with identifying numbers or license numbers. At the end of each year, revise this list and send it to your lawyer. This very useful exercise should be done by everyone and is an excellent reminder of how precious life is, and how we should allow death to be our best counselor.

Practice—Healing Through Pain

Each year billions and billions of dollars are spent on medicines which have no other function except that of being pain killers. On entering a pharmacy we always find row after row of headache pills and pain removers. Most people, especially Americans, consider pain an evil which must be removed or escaped from as soon as possible.

Actually, pain is in itself something good. It is a valuable pointer telling us that something has gone wrong that needs attention. When we focus that attention, the healing powers of our body dramatically increase. As that happens, pain decreases or stops entirely because it has succeeded in drawing needed attention.

The following are ways of doing this.

1. Focus your attention on the center of pain. Carefully note how the pain increases or decreases in intensity. With your finger or a pencil

and paper, make a graph of the pain, moving upward for an increase, downward for a decrease, or on a straight line when pain is steady. You will find that the pain will gradually decrease because of this entire attention to it.

2. Focus attention on your breathing. Imagine that your outgoing breathstream/energy is directed to the pain center. Repeat this with each breath. A mantra may be added for increased effectiveness such as "Come, Holy Spirit" on the in-breath and "Heal me/us with your love" on the out-breath. For increased focus and effect one of the following may be used: (a) with your eyes closed, imagine that a healing "laser" beam goes from each of your eyes to the pain center; (b) with your finger slowly describe a circle around the painful area. I used this method once after a painful operation. I was surprised by the dramatic, rapid healing that took place. The doctors and nurses were surprised that the usual post-operative pain relievers were not needed.

Points for group or class discussion as well as individual reflection:

1. What signs of death have you noticed during the past week? How can they help promote a more vibrant life?

2. If death is the ultimate full STOP sign, what are the little STOP signs of daily life? How can we use them to advance in personal growth?

3. What is the function of pain in the quest for integration? What are some practical ways to use pain as an approach to total health?

Annotated Bibliography For Further Reading

Burghardt, W., *Seasons That Laugh Or Weep* (Ramsey, N.J.: Paulist, 1984). Meditations on the seasons of life in human living.

Hellwig, M., *What Are They Saying About Death and Human Hope?* (Ramsey, N.J.: Paulist, 1978). An explanation of modern theologians' views about life and death in a Christian context.

Sullender, R.S., *Grief and Growth* (Ramsey, N.J.: Paulist, 1985). This book is written to provide resources for emotional and spiritual growth in times of pain, loss and bereavement.

10

The Secret of Jesus—Part I

The only real way to close the separating space between ourselves and others is through the deep attention that comes from "passionate" living. The most effective way to arrive at this is through a deep sense of identification with other people, and even with all living beings. In this way we can truly experience what it means to be one-in-all and *all in one,* and act according. There are many indications in the Gospels that this sense of identification was the special secret of Jesus himself.

Jesus once gave a short summary statement of the best means to personal growth found in all the Bible. In his Sermon on the Mount he declared, "Do unto others whatever you would wish them to do to you. This sums up the law and the prophets" (Mt 7:12). When Jesus said this, he was not giving a cold detached principle or idea. He was merely putting in words what had become an essential part of his own life-style. It was a keen, deeply felt sense of identification with other people. He could sense the problems, feelings, joys and sorrows of other people as his own. He could step into their shoes and experience life as they did.

Let us take some examples from the Gospels to see how Jesus did this in practice, even in the most difficult and desperate situations.

1. The supreme untouchable and outcast of those days was the leper. The law declared that leprosy made people continually ritually unclean. This meant they could take part in no social or religious gathering. Uncleanness was considered contagious so no one could touch them or come near them. They lived outside villages, often in cemeteries. They were like the living dead. Along with this they had the horrible feeling of loneliness and rejection from their own families and friends. Jesus had a deep feeling of what all this meant. The Gospel of Mark notes that he had sorrow and compassion in his heart (1:40). He knew that to be untouched and unloved was the greatest human suffering, so he actually

touched the leper and restored him to health. Then he gave the practical directions as to how he could be restored once more to the community. Jesus felt the sense of identification with the sick and afflicted so much that he could later say, "I was sick and you visited me" (Mt 25:36).

2. Another example is that of children. In the business and so-called man's world these are the unproductive and neglected persons. Yet Jesus said, "Unless you turn and become like children, you will never enter the kingdom of heaven" (Mt 18:3). In Jewish tradition, a favorite figure of the messianic age was that of children playing joyfully and without fear in the streets of Jerusalem (Zech 8:5). Jesus took special time to show his understanding and feeling of identification with children. On one occasion (Mk 10:13–16) young mothers were bringing little children to Jesus so he could lay his hand on them and bless them. Jesus' disciples were concerned that the Master had more important things to do—the sick to be healed, the urgent need to preach the kingdom of God. So they tried to stop the long procession and keep the children away. The Gospel of Mark takes special note of Jesus' emotions. He was really angry about this and said to them, "Let the little children come to me, and do not hinder them. It is to such as these that the kingdom of God belongs." Then the Gospel of Mark adds a beautiful intimate touch to the story: Jesus put his arms around each child, embracing each one and imparting a blessing.

On another occasion (Mk 9:34–37) the disciples were arguing with one another as to who was the greatest or most important in their group. They meant this in the sense of whoever was closest to Jesus and the best leader. Jesus heard about this and called his disciples together to make a special point. He sat down with all his disciples in a circle around him. He said to them, "The one who wishes to be first must become least and servant of all." Then he took a little child and placed his arms around it to show who were really closest to his heart. Then, in a very striking way he identified himself with children in these words: "Anyone who receives a little child in my name receives me." It is not surprising, then, that when Jesus came to Jerusalem for the last time and visited the temple, it was children who met him and sang out: "Hosanna to the Son of David" (Mt 21:15). As a result, the chief priests of the temple demanded that Jesus silence them. Jesus replied to them in the words of Scripture, Psalm 8, saying, "Did you never read this, 'From the speech of children and infants you have framed a hymn of praise' "?

3. Another important area of identification was with women. Their clearly defined roles in those days made it difficult for men to associate with them as equals or friends and understand their feelings. Jesus does not hesitate to speak out openly about the matter that caused women the most suffering and embarrassment. In those days, divorce was a male prerogative. A woman was regarded as part of the husband's household or property which he could dispose of by a written bill. Jesus restored marriage to a position of a personal covenant or relationship that cannot be dealt with in terms of property (Mt 19:4–9). In doing so, he appealed to the text of Genesis 2:24, "For this reason, a man leaves his father and mother and clings to his wife and they become one flesh." The word "cling" in this text signifies in Hebrew a personal union or covenant. Jesus' attitude toward women was put into practice by his own actions. Contrary to the practice of his time, he accepted women disciples. An example is Martha and Mary in Luke 10. Contrary to custom, he greeted and spoke to women—even strangers in public. This caused a reaction among his disciples, on one occasion, who were wondering why he was speaking alone with a Samaritan woman (Jn 4:27).

It is also surprising that Jesus does a number of things that were ordinarily considered the special role of women. He washes the feet of the disciples (Jn. 13)—which was ordinarily done by slaves in a large house or by women in a small home. He also cooks and sets a meal before his disciples (Jn 21:9–10). Serving at table was ordinarily considered a woman's role. Yet Jesus describes himself in this way: "I am in the midst of you as one who serves" (Lk 22:27). The Gospel of Luke notes that women followed Jesus on his journey just as the twelve disciples did (8:2). Some of them, from rich families, helped support him and his disciples. Women, in return, responded to his attention and understanding in an extraordinary way. They were the only ones, according to Matthew, Mark and Luke, who remained with him at the foot of the cross until he died. They stayed on when everyone else fled in fear. They alone came to the tomb on Easter morn and were the first to see the risen Lord.

4. Jesus identified with suffering and pain. Those people who have a deep sense of identification with others feel a strong compassion for their suffering, especially for their failures. Jesus himself was deeply moved and cried at the death of Lazarus, the brother of Martha and Mary (Jn 11:33–35). When Jesus approached Jerusalem for the last time and

saw the city from a distance, he began to cry as he thought of the suffering and destruction that would come to the city because they would accept violent revolutionary leaders, instead of himself, a Messiah of peace (Lk 20:41–44).

Jesus knew too that sin, failure and guilt cause people some of their most excruciating suffering. From the very beginning of his public career, he identified himself in a very special way with sinners. He went down into the Jordan River with a group of repentant sinners, publicly identifying himself with them, being baptized with them. Jesus shocked the religious leaders of his time by frequently sharing his meals with tax collectors and sinners. When asked why he did this, he replied, "It is not those who are healthy who need a physician but those who are sick. I have not come to call the just but sinners" (Mt 9:13). Indeed the complete forgiveness of sin was considered so tremendous a matter that it was considered reserved for the last days of history. Only in God's final intervention in the world would he freely and completely forgive sin. So we can understand why many religious leaders were completely shocked when Jesus proclaimed that this final time of complete forgiveness was right here and now. When Jesus told the paralytic that his sins were forgiven, the scribes and Pharisees were so shocked that they said that Jesus was blaspheming—"Who can forgive sins but God alone?" (Mk 2:7). Jesus' association with sinners made such an impact that his enemies called him "a wine drinker and glutton, a friend of tax collectors and sinners" (Mt 11:19).

Matthew sees Jesus' identification with others as a central theme of the Gospel. At Jesus' baptism, John the Baptist was surprised and shocked to see Jesus come to him, asking for baptism along with a group of sinners. The Baptist tried to stop him from doing so and said, "It is I who ought to be baptized by you, and yet you come to me" (Mt 3:14). Jesus, however, replied that it was fitting that he should do so to fulfill God's purpose. Matthew sees Jesus' miracles and compassion for the sick in terms of the humble servant of the Lord in Isaiah 53 who took upon himself the affliction and even the sins of others. After Jesus cures a crowd of sick and possessed, Matthew notes as following: This was to fulfill the prophecy of Isaiah: "It was our infirmities he bore, our suffering he endured" (8:17).

In fact, the author considers Jesus' identification with others so important that it becomes the subject of the last judgment scene in 25:31–

46, which summarizes all of Jesus' teaching. There the just are welcomed with joy into heaven by the king, who is Jesus, Son of Man. They are then told the reason for their triumph in these words: "I was hungry and you gave me to eat, I was thirsty and you gave me to drink. I was a stranger and you made me welcome, naked and you clothed me, sick and you visited me, in prison and you came to see me." The virtuous then asked when they saw him hungry, thirsty, a stranger, naked, sick or in prison. Then the king announces the supreme theme of Jesus' identification with others: "Amen I say to you, as long as you did it to one of these the least of my brothers, you did it to me." Notice how strongly the emphasis is made—first a sixfold repetition of the theme in the form "I was hungry, thirsty, etc.," and then a full repetition of the entire six in the question of the just.

On the contrary, there is no specific list of sins to condemn the unjust. It is lack of identification and insensitivity to the needy that is the root cause. Here again the sixfold repetition is placed in a negative form repeated in the question of the unjust, concluded by the negative summary, "As long as you did *not* do it to one of these, the least of my brothers, you did not do it to me." In all the theme is repeated twenty-four times plus the two conclusions. Matthew could not emphasize in a stronger way the central theme of Jesus' identification with others.

Suggestions for Practice

In daily life, we can more easily identify with others as we see or imagine ourselves with the same suffering, anger, worry or emotion that they have at some incident or time in our life. For example, we might at first be upset by seeing a child steal, tell a lie, or use rough language. We can always recall an incident when we did the same or almost the same thing. Then we can try to understand and identify by seeing ourself in others. When we do this, we see them no longer as objects, but as persons, with all the feelings, problems, worries and emotions that we have. In our daily journal we can take special note of how we have been able to identify with others during the day.

Next let us look at the secret of Jesus in reference to the inner goals and directions of his life.

In everything we do in life, it is important to know two things:

Where are we going and how are we going to get there? An important part of the whole meaning of life is the question (1) of the goals we have in life and (2) how we are going to attain them. If we asked Jesus what he wanted to do in life, he would simply answer, *"To do the will of my Father."* If we asked what this will was, he would further specify with the answer, *"To make his kingdom come."* Indeed the phrase "kingdom of God" is repeated over a hundred times in the Gospels. The dominant concern of all Jesus' life is the *kingdom of God.*

But what is the kingdom of God? It is simply a world where everyone obeys God as king and does what he wants. It is the world God wants it to be, a world of peace, justice, love and oneness. The Hebrew word *shalom* or peace summarizes the kingdom of God. It is a world of peace and goodness where all the barriers that separate people and nations are broken down, whether social, economic, racial or religious. The apostle Paul summed it all up when he wrote to the Galatians (3:28): "There is neither Jew nor Greek, there is neither slave nor free, there is neither male nor female; for you are all one in Christ Jesus." Notice the expression *you are all one.* It is taken from the greatest and most repeated name of God in the Old Testament—which is THE ONE. This is found in the famous passage in Deuteronomy 6:4–9: *"Hear, O Israel, the Lord your God is One.* And you shall love the Lord your God with your whole heart, your whole soul, your whole mind and your whole strength." This prayer was to be repeated over and over again each day—at home, while traveling, while at work. Later it became the great central prayer of Judaism repeated three times each day in the synagogue and by every pious Jew. This oneness of God is not just philosophical. God is one because he creates one*ness* in all that he does. He originally made the world one harmonious family and works continually to restore it to such. The prophet Zechariah predicts a day when there will be one God and *one people* (14:9).

Jesus taught that the kingdom of God was beginning right *here and now.* His first concern was to break down the separating barriers between people and restore this oneness. When a rich young man wanted to be his disciple, his answer was simple: "Go sell what you have and give to the poor, and you will have treasure in heaven, and come follow me" (Mk 10:21). The economic barriers between rich and poor must be broken by sharing. Then there were the barriers between the so-called "clean" and "unclean"—the ritual disqualifications that kept so many people from social gatherings. Jesus broke them down by touching the sick and healing them. We saw the example of the leper in the last section. We have seen how he took special pains to tear down the walls of separation between men and women, between Jews and stranger Gentiles. His own little group of twelve which shared a common purse brought together even fishermen, a hated tax collector and a former Zealot.

Practice and Exercises

What drains so much of our energy is worry, anxiety about future events in life—most of which never even happen to us. Jesus gave us the cure for this in presenting the only meaningful goal of life—which is to work for God's kingdom by prayer and action. In the Sermon on the Mount, he sums up his own action and goal in these words: *Seek first his kingdom and his righteousness and all these things shall be yours as well* (6:33). In other words when the *kingdom of God* becomes the supreme and over-riding goal of life, everything else falls in proper perspective and comes to us as a gift and surprise rather than as a demand. Jesus' central commitment in life to the kingdom was very much like the commitment to be a *world citizen* which is a first consequence of a deep understanding of the oneness of the universe. We can now better appreciate why Jesus would repeat again and again the mantra. ''Thy kingdom come'' from the Lord's Prayer, and why he asked his disciples to pray in the same manner.

But where did Jesus draw the tremendous energies needed for such a selfless identification with others and such a complete dedication to the kingdom? Here is the second part of the secret of Jesus: his deep sense of identification with God. The most surprising statements of all are found in the Gospel of John where Jesus proclaims, ''I and the Father are one'' (10:30). Some of the bystanders were so shocked by this statement that they looked for stones to throw at him as a witness to blasphemy. It is even more startling that Jesus does not reserve such statements to himself. He even prays that his disciples be likewise aware of their oneness with the Father: ''That they may be one: even as you Father are in me and I in you'' (17:21). Jesus' purpose is not to stand apart or above but to share what he has with others to such an extent that he can say, ''I am in my Father, and you in me, and I in you'' (14:21).

The awareness of this divine identification is a most powerful means to energize our daily lives. Yet with our own memories of past failure and weakness it is hard to accept that we are *all in one* and *one in all,* the way that Jesus spoke of himself in the Gospel of John. A very effective mantra to help in this direction is the very assertion of Jesus, "I am in you and you are in me" (14:21). Breathe in the words "I am in you," then breathe out "You are in me." This can be repeated again and again in meditation and in the company of others.

Points for group or class discussion as well as individual reflection:

1. What was Jesus' secret of "passionate living"? In what way do you think it could become a reality in your own life?

2. What is meant by identification with others in accord with Jesus' model in the Gospel? Why is this such a quick and direct path to personal growth? How can we make steady progress in real identification with others?

11

The Secret of Jesus—Part II

In anything we do in life it is important to know two things: where we are going and how we are going to get there. The first part for Jesus— where are we going—was summed up in his dedication to the kingdom of God. The second part is very practical: how to get there. Here again our best model is that of Jesus. Jesus himself chose to imitate God, his own Father. This was also the supreme ideal of Jewish piety. But how could a person imitate God? The pious Jew did this by studying Scripture and watching how God acted in history. What type of a God was he? A valuable key was found in the introduction to the ten commandments in Exodus 20:1, ''I am the Lord your God who brought you out of the land of Egypt, that house of bondage.''

In other words, God's great quality is that of a liberator—he takes the first step to go out to a people who are slaves and doomed to death in Egypt. This initiative is called *grace*. It is unexpected, unmerited and due to God's unconditional love for his people. It was this quality of God that Jesus wanted to imitate. This is why he felt that his special mission was to go to the outcasts of Israel, those most desperately in need. Consequently, he took a special interest in women, tax collectors, sinners, the sick, and the mentally ill. This mission to the outcasts was not just a task or drive on his part. The unique qualities of this love were, first, its unconditional nature and, second, the renunciation of power or nonviolence that accompanied it.

First of all, it was an unconditional love—the model of Jesus was God's own great universal love for all people, the good as well as the bad, the just as well as the unjust. It is well expressed in the Sermon on the Mount: ''that you may be children of your Father who is in heaven, for he makes his sun rise on the evil and the good, and sends his rain on the just and on the unjust'' (Mt 5:45). This type of unconditional love

was especially highlighted by Jesus' directive, "Love your enemies."
For a Jew of the time, *the* hated enemy was the Roman oppressor, and
whoever collaborated with him. The closest and most disliked collabo-
rator of Rome was the Jewish tax collector who bought his office from
the Romans and then used Roman power to collect whatever he could
from his own people, especially the poor.

We can imagine the surprise and shock of Jesus' disciples when he
walked into a tax collector's office—that of a man called Levi or Matthew—and said, "Come follow me" (Mt 9:9). And we can imagine the
joyful enthusiasm of Levi and other tax collectors and sinners like him
as Jesus associated with them as equals and friends, accepting them as
they were. Mark notes, "As he sat at table in his house, many tax collectors and sinners were sitting with Jesus and his disciples, for there
were many who followed him" (2:15).

The second group of so-called "enemies" were persons who had
injured or hurt others economically, or even personally. Jesus knew and
felt this keenly in his own life. Judas was a man he had personally selected to be part of his core community. He had even entrusted Judas
with a very responsible office, that of holding the community purse and
distributing funds for their own support and for the poor. Judas was his
associate in his journeys and mission, his companion at all his meals,
one of those who slept by his side at night. Yet Jesus knew he was con-
spiring with Jewish authorities to hand him over. We can imagine no
deeper hurt that one person could possibly give to another. Yet despite
this, Jesus continued to love him and even showed him special signs of
affection. He took care to hand him a choice morsel at the Last Supper.
He kissed him with affection when he came with soldiers to arrest him.
When Jesus said, "Love your enemies," he was speaking from his heart
about a pure, unconditional love that he had learned from his own experience.

A special characteristic of this type of love was a very active, thoroughly non-violent response to injuries or insults on the part of others.
It was not passive acceptance or tolerance, but an active response that
even brought a positive benefit to the instigator. From a human standpoint, this attitude had an almost ridiculous or laughable element to it,
because it was so strikingly different from the ordinary way people act
in anger and retaliation. Thus Jesus would say (if we place it in a modern
idiom): "If someone wishes to go to court and take your coat, let him

take your trousers as well'' (Mt 5:40). The Roman occupation army was constantly requistioning men to build roads or carry their heavy equipment. Most men did so in angry reluctance with a curse under their breath. Jesus said, ''If anyone forces you to go one mile, go with him two'' (Mt 5:41). Imagine the surprise of a Roman soldier if a Jew would respond with love and a smile, offering to do even more out of good will. Such was Jesus' way to deal with violence and imposition. Once again it was not a matter of a philosopher's counsel, but something that was part of his own life-style. When soldiers came to arrest Jesus in the Garden of Olives, they did not have to search him out; he came forth to deliver himself into their hands. When his disciples drew their swords and tried to resist, Jesus told them, ''Put your swords back into place, for all those who take the sword will perish by the sword (Mt 26:52).

Notes for Practice

Teaching on unconditional love—even of enemies like Judas who have hurt the most—seems impossible. Indeed it is rare to see it, and so beautiful when it happens because it is a pure manifestation of God's own unconditional love. And because it is God's love, it is a great gift of the Holy Spirit who alone can give it to us. As Paul writes, ''God's love has been poured into our hearts through the Holy Spirit who has been given us'' (Rom 5:5).

Jesus himself told us how to make a decisive breakthrough in this area. In the words of Luke, it is as follows: ''Do good to those who hate you, bless those who curse you, pray for those who abuse you.'' In this verse there are three very active approaches: (1) performing some active good deed for someone who has hurt or wronged you in some way; (2) a prayer for them; (3) sending them a blessing. A very simple yet dramatically effective way to do this is to recall a person for whom there is somehow a bitter memory in our heart. Picture the incident and feel its effects. Concentrate on your breath. Breathe the person in and out through your body until the feeling of hurt diminishes or disappears. Now recall the Holy Spirit mantra: ''Come, Holy Spirit—fill our hearts with love.'' On your in-breath say silently, ''Come, Holy Spirit,'' on the out-breath, ''Fill our hearts with love.'' Keep repeating this until you actually experience warmth and love for that person instead of bitterness and unpleasant feelings. When this happens, thank the Holy Spirit for the gift of love—your whole life can dramatically change to an outflow of love and happiness when you have been able to do this. This especially applies to people who have formerly been close to us, but toward whom we now experience separating emotions. This practice can be briefly renewed each night before going to sleep—forgiving from our hearts anyone who has hurt or injured us during that day. This is the advice given by Ephesians 4:26—"Do not let the sun go down on your anger."

Jesus could well be called "a mystic in action." Although he spent many quiet hours in prayer and communion with God, the greatest part of his life was spent in crowds, contacts with people, traveling in what most people would call an active, busy life. How could he be close to God in the midst of so much activity? The secret of Jesus was not to withdraw from the world, but to penetrate deeper within the world and find God's presence within the people, events and realities of each day. Jesus had actually learned this secret from a profound Jewish spirituality found in the Bible.

I might illustrate this by again citing the experience of driving along a California highway and seeing a large billboard advertisement that caught my attention. It pictured a large pizza and underneath it was the caption: "Not by bread alone does man exist but by Straw Hat Pizza." I recognized a play on the words of Scripture, quoted by Jesus: "Not by bread alone does man exist but by every word that comes from the mouth of God." The advertisement brought out that common bread can have a deeper meaning; the biblical text tells us that this deeper meaning of bread is found in God, the source of all nourishment. In other words, when we break bread, we can eat it at a very deep level and taste God himself, the source of all nourishment. There is indeed a deep inner level and symbolism in all reality. When we perceive this, the universe becomes literally *transubstantiated*—God himself is found beneath the ordinary commonplace realities of each day.

At the center of Jewish spirituality was the importance of being aware of this deep level of reality by recognizing and acknowledging God's presence and activity in the world. This was done in two principal areas, that of nature and that of history. It was built on the conviction that the whole world was a theater and manifestation of God's presence and activity. This conviction is found in the vision of Isaiah the prophet in chapter 6, where the angels proclaim, "Holy, holy, holy Lord God of Hosts. Heaven and earth are filled with your glory." An example of

God's manifestation in nature is found in Psalm 8. The Psalm begins by declaring that God's name or manifestation in the universe is so evident that even little children recognize it with wonder and sing praise to God; the earth, sun and stars are not cold feelingless objects but are like rays of his goodness, warmth and presence. The psalmist writes, "When I look at your heavens, the work of your fingers, the moon and the stars which you set in place—what is man that you are mindful of him?" The psalmist does not see human beings in isolation in the universe but interconnected with all creatures. To express this, he divides all living beings into four categories: the wild and tame animals, those that dwell in the sea, and those that fly in the air: "You have put all things under his feet, all sheep and oxen, and also the beasts of the field, the birds in the air, and the fish in the sea."

The second area of God's presence and activity is that of history. This is so pervasive and evident throughout the Bible that few examples are needed. God is preeminently a God of history, as in the prologue to the ten commandments: "I am the Lord your God who brought you out of the land of Egypt, that house of bondage" (Ex 20:1). In fact, the very name of God is often linked with his people. The revelation name of God is Yahweh—which is from the verb to be. God constantly declares throughout the Bible: "I will be with you." He is a God who is present with his people and in his people, guiding them through history. The celebration and remembrance of the presence of God was not reserved for sabbath worship and feasts; it was part and parcel of daily life. It was done in the form of a blessing or recognition when God's presence was especially manifest in some way.

The first volume of the Jewish talmud is called *Berakot* which means "blessings." It enumerates hundreds of occasions for blessings and formulas for them. This was the most frequent type of prayer each day. The ideal was that expressed in Psalm 34:1, "I will bless the Lord at all times, his praise shall continually be in my mouth." A prominent rabbi once commented on this Psalm and said that a person who did not bless God at least one hundred times a day was like a heathen or pagan! Although blessings could be composed spontaneously in one's own words, there were fixed forms that could be used for the events of each day. The blessing always began with the expression "Blessed be Thou, O Lord our God, King of the World"—followed by the particular reason for the blessing. Some examples: sleep was considered a gift of God—

yet close to death. To awake in the morning was to be born again and live a new life; hence the Blessing: "Blessed be Thou, O Lord Our God, King of the World who raises up the dead." On opening the eyes: "who opens the eyes of the blind." On hearing the first sound: "who gives hearing to the deaf." On putting on clothes: "who clothes the naked." On taking bread or food, "who brings forth bread from the earth." Note the reference to God as the source of nourishment—the one "who brings forth bread from the earth." Since this blessing is very ancient, it is probably the same one recited by Jesus at the Last Supper when he took bread and pronounced a blessing. Blessings had their own little ritual: the eyes were raised to heaven and the head bowed at the name of God. Those who heard a blessing responded with the words, "Blessed be He—Blessed be His Name." Jesus took this traditional form of prayer and used it to remember God many thousands of times in his life.

Notes for Practice

If prayer is to be meaningful, it should be linked to the realities and events of daily life. Traditional Jews and charismatic Christians have retained the verbal form of blessing or praise in daily life. Yet the essence or root is the remembrance of God, which can be non-verbal. It is the secret of finding the extraordinary in the ordinary. Even a piece of bread can be the occasion of mystical union with God. It is thus a way to "transubstantiate" the universe and recover a deep sense of wonder—a sense that is being rapidly lost in our modern world. To those who have this attitude, miracles are not isolated events. Everything is miraculous if we look beneath the surface. Only some are more evident than others. Without memory and remembrance of God, his name becomes dead and meaningless.

However, there is another essential aspect to Jesus' belief in a God of history. The Gospels refer on almost every page to the fulfillment of Scripture. Jesus believed that Scripture was not only a book of the past, but that it was God's plan for the future as well. As we have seen, the goal of Jesus' life was the kingdom of God and all that this meant. For him, all of history had a direction and movement for the kingdom of God. This direction came from God—what is called Divine Providence. Jesus trusted in this and found new energy and power in all that he did as a result of it. He was conscious and aware that if God had planned the kingdom of God, he would also give him the power he needed to do his part in making it a reality.

An example of Jesus' consciousness of the divine plan at work in his ministry is found in the story of his meeting with the Samaritan woman. The Gospel of John notes that Jesus was tired and exhausted as he rested by the well of Jacob in Samaria (4:6). Meanwhile his disciples went to the village to buy food and refreshments. When they returned, they expected the tired Master to eagerly dine with them. Instead he said to them, "I have food to eat of which you do not know" (4:33). The disciples were puzzled and asked one another if someone had brought him food. Jesus however told them, "My food is to do the will of him who sent me, and to accomplish his work." It is interesting that Gandhi and other great men and women of history have found boundless energy in the same mysterious source. When asked why he risked his life and took public stands with such energy and confidence, Gandhi replied that no one else in his particular situation could do what he had to do. He was confident that God's plan and all of history were behind him.

Points for Practice

We have already seen the importance of being and living in the here-and-now, but we can now notice a new and exciting dimension. Once we have set our sights and the goal of our life on the kingdom of God, we have lined ourself up as well with the great purpose and direction of God in all the universe. This brings to bear a new energy and power at work in our life—one that we can trust and tap as we need to. Just like Jesus, we can feel that we are fulfilling Scripture, or the plan of God. In our daily journal it would be well to take special note of threads of this plan running together. A good hint in this direction is to look in our day for all the actions and events that have led to oneness, peace, justice and the loving service of others. These are specific signs of the movement of the kingdom of God.

The second special area of God's presence is in people and nature. We have already studied God's action in people, so let us go to Jesus' awareness of the Spirit in nature. In the Sermon on the Mount we saw that God's action in nature is a sign of his unconditional love. Jesus said, "Be children of your Father who is in heaven, for he makes his sun rise on the evil and on the good, and sends rain on the just and on the unjust"

(Mt 5:45). Also, God's loving care shows itself in the animal world which Jesus told us to observe: "Look at the birds of the air. They neither sow nor reap nor gather into barns, and yet your heavenly Father feeds them" (Mt 6:26). Jesus also reminded us to observe the beauty of even wild flowers in the field as a showplace of God's care in the smallest details of creation. He said, "Behold the lilies of the field, how they grow; they never toil nor spin, yet I tell you even Solomon in all his glory was not arrayed like one of these" (Mt 6:30).

Some exercises and points for practice: Jesus spent many hours in quiet communion with God in the atmosphere of nature. He would relax in their little sailboat crossing the Lake of Galilee. He often climbed a mountain to have time for silence and prayer. A favorite spot—a special place of prayer and rest—was a grove of olive trees near Jerusalem. In life, we often need times of peace and communion with God in the quiet of nature, whether it is the ocean, the forest, or the mountains. We need to recover our sense of oneness with the universe, whether in plants, animals, other human beings, rocks, stones, mountains, sun, air, stars at night. The following is an exercise that can be used to help break our estrangement from the universe.

Take a tree for example—stand up and lean against it. Now close your eyes and try to identify with it as much as you can, making the tree's "feelings" your own. Have the tree be an observer of you. How does it feel to have roots in the ground, leaves in the sun and air? How does it feel to sway with the wind? See if you can feel as much like a tree as possible. When you are finished, try to see what meaning you can draw from this experience. This same exercise can be done for plants, flowers, a waterfall, animals, etc.

Another exercise is an inward journey to God in the universe through our imagination and identification with nature. After some restful awareness of your breathing, close your eyes. Imagine you are in a familiar meadow. You see a flower in the distance and go over to it. (Take time for each part of the meditation so your imagination can have full freedom.) Now imagine you are the flower. First identify with the flower petal itself as it absorbs the sun and sways in the breeze. Now feel the source of liquid energy coming up through the stem from the ground to the petal. Now move down the stem to the roots. Notice the hundreds of fibers moving in all directions to bring water and nourishment to you. Now imagine that the roots broaden and go deeper and deeper into the earth—five feet—ten feet—twenty feet—fifty feet, etc. (Give time to each element in the meditation.) Now imagine the roots spreading out all through the earth searching for water, nourishment and energy—then picture the roots going beyond the earth to the warmth and energy of the sun—then to the millions of stars and suns that form our own galaxy, the milky way—to the far-off millions of galaxies that make up the universe. Finally retrace your path gradually to the flower, bringing back every source of energy that is found in the universe to the stem and blossom in the form of a precious nectar that gives life and nourishment to the flower. Now imagine a person coming over to look at the flower (which is you) and see what happens. When you are ready, open your eyes and reflect on what this experience meant to you.

Points for group or class discussion as well as individual reflection:

1. What is meant by unconditional love as taught by Jesus? Can we love others according to this model and yet dislike them? What should we do if we find ourselves with a feeling of dislike or antipathy toward others?

2. How did Jesus, Gandhi and other great men and women tap into limitless energy through their belief in a God of history? How can we do the same?

3. How was Jesus a mystic despite a very active life? What practical suggestions would you have for people to become "mystics in action"?

Annotated Bibliography for Further Reading (For Chapters 10–11)

Grassi, J., *God Makes Me Laugh: A New Approach to Luke* (Wilmington, Del.: M. Glazier, 1986). Luke's understanding of Jesus' unique approach to teaching through laughter, humor and comic paradoxes.

Grassi, J., *Broken Bread and Broken Bodies: The Lord's Supper and World Hunger* (N.Y.: Orbis, 1985). The Lord's Supper/Eucharist sums up, expresses and renews Jesus' understanding of the Gospel as good news to the poor and hungry.

Nolan, A., *Jesus Before Christianity* (N.Y.: Orbis, 1978). A very fine presentation of the challenge of Jesus earthly mission in light of the social, political and economic background of the times.

12

The Vision of Paul

Identification with Christ

The letters of Paul occupy more than one-quarter of the whole New Testament. If to this we add the Acts of the Apostles, written essentially about him, we obtain a figure between one-third and one-half of the New Testament. If we consider Paul's influence, he is the person almost entirely responsible for the beginning of Gentile Christianity—which is all that has come down to the present day. Yet his importance is even greater from the personal and spiritual standpoint. St. Augustine calls him the "man who knew Christ best." And yet as far as we know, he never met the earthly Jesus. What then was the secret of his enormous vitality and influence? This secret is that of his identification with Christ, fortunately a secret we can all share with him. Paul expressed this identity in the words of Galatians 2:20, "It is no longer I who live, but Christ who lives in me," and again in Philippians 1:21, "For to me, to live is Christ, and to die is gain." This identity with Christ meant the sharing of a new divine life filled with energy and love that he could not possibly have attained by his own efforts.

What then was Paul's root experience of identification? It is something we can all share as our greatest source of strength, so we can say with Paul, "I can do all things in him who strengthens me" (Phil 4:13). Paul describes this simply and powerfully in Romans 6 where he understands baptism not as a solitary experience from the past but one that enters into everyday life experience. He writes, "Do you not know that all of us who have been baptized into Christ Jesus were baptized into his death? We were buried therefore with him by baptism into death so that as Christ was raised from the dead by the glory of the Father, we too might walk in newness of life" (6:3–4). This baptismal experience and identification with Christ has two parts: the first is the stripping off of our old clothes. These old clothes symbolize our previous life dominated by all kinds of desires and attachments that lead to sin—really a separation between ourselves, God and other people. Baptism means becoming supremely like Christ in dying as he did—willfully separating himself from the limitations of earthly life. So Paul writes, "We know that our old self was crucified with him so that the sinful body might be destroyed, and we might no longer be enslaved to sin" (6:6). The second step is union and identification with Christ in his new risen life. After being thoroughly immersed with him in the waters of death in the tomb, we can emerge with him, thoroughly cleansed, and put on new clothes, symbolizing the new life and identity we have entered into. It is the life of Christ himself dominated by love and the Spirit. Henceforth as new persons, we acquire a new name—that of Christ. The word Christian is actually a name—in its root meaning it signifies one who belongs to Christ.

This new life is not just a general principle but a complete new life-style—that of Jesus himself. This is what Paul means by "walking in newness of life" (6:4). "Walking" in the biblical sense means a direction or movement of our whole body and self. It might be called a duplication of the life of Jesus himself. Paul calls this a life which is led according to a certain rule which he calls the "law of Christ" (Gal 6:2).

If we look carefully at this law of Christ or rule of love as embodied in Paul, we will see a close identification with the life-style of Jesus as summarized by the Sermon on the Mount. Jesus had said, "Love your enemies, do good to those who hate you, and bless those who curse you" (Lk 6:20–28). In writing to the Corinthians, Paul describes how he had experienced insults and curses and how he responded. He writes, "When reviled, we bless" (1 Cor 4:12). His greatest suffering came at the hands of fellow Jews. In 2 Corinthians 11:24, he writes, "Five times I received at the hands of the Jews the forty lashes, less one." Yet at the same time, these Jews have the closest place in his heart as we see in the beginning of Romans 9. Jesus had taught that true love was non-conditional and non-judgmental when he said, "Judge not and you shall not be judged" (Mt 7:1). Paul echoes the same theme in Galatians 6:2–5, where he tells the Galatians to bear one another's burden, forgive and understand, rather than judge. Jesus' special concern and mission was to the outcast and weak of Israel. Paul gives his special attention to the weak in the community, especially those weak in conscience, basing this on imitation of Christ; he writes in Romans 15:1, "We who are strong ought to bear with the failings of the weak, and not to please ourselves: let each of us please his neighbor for his good, to edify him. For Christ did not please himself." Again, to the Corinthians he writes (1 Cor 9:22): "To the weak I become weak, that I might win the weak. I have become all things to all men." Jesus had taught in the Sermon on the Mount not to resist the evildoer, but to win over others by love, avoiding lawsuits (5:39). Writing to the Corinthians, Paul was shocked to hear they were having lawsuits before pagan judges. He advised them either to settle them in the Christian community or to forgive and sustain injury willingly (1 Cor 6:11).

Paul had his own special way of renewing and strengthening his identification with Christ. We find this secret in Galatians 4:6, "Because you are sons, God has sent the Spirit of his Son into our hearts crying, '*Abba,* Father.' " Here it is especially interesting that Paul preserves an original Aramaic word, *Abba,* although he is writing in Greek to an audience that does not know Aramaic at all. This is because he wants to preserve, as part of Christian tradition and practice, the very word that Jesus himself had used in his own prayer. The Gospel of Mark tells us that Jesus prayed in his agony in the garden with the words, "*Abba,* Father, all things are possible to you" (Mk 14:36). Jesus used the word *Abba* because it was the special intimate affectionate term used by children to speak to their earthly fathers. It was never used to address God. In prayer to God the more formal Hebrew word for father was used. To use *Abba* for God would be equivalent to referring to God as "dad", a term in English used only of earthly fathers. The word *Abba* was the most precious word in Jesus' language. It summarized his own special, unique loving relationship to God that enabled him to speak to him with absolute confidence.

We can see then that the climax of Paul's identification with Christ was to say with him, in reverence and affection, "*Abba,* Father," to God. Here in Galatians, he mentions it as well as in Romans 8:16 as a most precious privilege of a Christian—one who bears Jesus' name. It is a gift and privilege made possible only by the gift of the very Spirit of Jesus, the Spirit of God.

Notes for Practice: Paul himself suggests an important practice in the above use of "Abba, Father." It meant so much to him that we find the term "Father" used over one hundred times in his letters. It is essential to go to the roots of what *Abba* meant to Jesus. In the agony in the garden, when Jesus prayed *"Abba,* Father," he added, "All things are possible to you" (Mk 14:36). In other words, *Abba* means radical obedience to God despite what seems absolutely impossible from a human standpoint—the ability to face the cross for the sake of the kingdom of God. So the great secret of prayer is the simple direction of our heart along with absolute confidence that God is truly *Abba* and *must* answer us as a kind, loving Father. There is no other possibility. In practice, then, when we pray, Jesus tells us to form in our minds an *image of* what we want as *already accomplished* or *happening:*

> Amen I say to you, whoever says to this mountain "Be taken up and cast into the sea," and does not doubt in his heart, but believes that what he says will come to pass, it will be done for him. Therefore I tell you, whatever you ask in prayer, believe that you receive it and you will (Mk 11:22–23).

Apply this text by imagining something you *really* need as already given to you. Repeat the confident image a few moments each day. You will be surprised to find out how quickly the image becomes a reality.

Returning to the Pauline theme of identification with Christ, Paul believed there were special solemn intense occasions for deepening this identification with Christ. This took place at what he called the supper of the Lord. He called it the supper of the Lord because it was a meal eaten at his command—in the way he wanted it eaten, in the way he wanted to be remembered. Hence it had a unique power all of its own. In writing to the Corinthians he carefully recalls the tradition of the Lord's supper:

> For I received from the Lord, what I also delivered to you, that the Lord Jesus on the night when he was betrayed took bread, and when he had given thanks, he broke it, and said: "This is my body which is for you. Do this in remembrance of me" (1 Cor 11:23–24).

Paul believed that these words signified a most intimate union with the person of Jesus. Eating the bread and absorbing it into the body signified union with Jesus so that his spirit and person became united to the believer. That is why he can speak in the strongest possible terms about this union and identification with Christ. In the same letter he writes, "The cup of blessing which we bless, is it not a participation, a sharing in the blood of Christ? The bread which we break, is it not a participation in the body of Christ" (10:16–17)? It is important that the Eucharist or supper of the Lord be a special time in life—a time reserved for the deepest moments of identification with Christ and through him to our brothers and sisters as well.

Meditation and Exercise

The following is a very effective form of meditation on this identification theme which can be repeated again and again. As an introduction, recall the promise of God in the Old Testament in the words of Ezekiel the prophet: "A new heart I will give you, and a new spirit I will put within you" (36:26). God is promising nothing less than a heart transplant which he himself will make possible. Now place yourself in a relaxed though alert position. Close your eyes—come in contact with your breathing—feel your breath all the way in and all the way out. Now imagine the heart of Christ—a heart burning with love and compassion, a heart filled with the great universal love of God. Imagine that heart expanding to include all the love of all fathers and mothers for their children (*pause*) the love of spouses and friends for one another (*pause*) imagine and picture the love of Christ for the sick, the downcast, the mentally ill (*pause*) *feel each step as much as possible* (*pause*) see it include the love for the sick and needy found in the compassionate hearts of people all around the world (*pause*) identify with his love for animals, birds, fish, plants (*pause*) see it included in the love found in great and sensitive people like Francis of Assisi and others you have known (*pause*) now imagine this heart expanding to include the hearts of all beings on earth (*pause*) then to include the other planets and the sun (*pause*) then the millions of stars in our own galaxy (*pause*) then to millions of other galaxies in the universe (*pause*) until it is the one great throbbing, loving pulsating heart of the universe. Now recall the promise of God in Ezekiel to give you a new heart.

See Jesus thinking of this promise and of you especially in the Last Supper as he says, "Eat this; this is my body." See Jesus giving over to you his body, especially his great loving heart as his special gift—to be your own heart, God's promised transplant of a new heart and spirit. Feel this as much as possible, and when you are ready, open your eyes and repeat your new name—that of Christ. Repeat the words of Paul: "I live now, not I, but Christ Jesus within me." Renew this identification exercise at least each week and especially before the Lord's supper. The heart meditation has been used for thousands of years in eastern and western meditation because of its unusual power. This is a Christian adaptation that has remarkable effects—because it is not just imaginary but *real*.

Community, Spirit and World

Christianity in the western world, as we have mentioned, is largely due to the dynamic work of one man, Paul, a former Jewish rabbi. It was due to his insights and energy that the Gospel was brought to the principal urban centers of the Roman empire. One very practical and effective dimension of his approach was the ability to start strong communities who were able to continue and grow after he had left them for new areas. What was the secret of his great success?

First of all, Paul was a team-worker. Except on rare occasions, he never traveled alone. This was a precedent established by Jesus himself, who traveled with the twelve, shared a common purse (Jn 12:6; 13:29) and when necessary sent his apostles out two by two (Mk 6:7). On Paul's first journey, he was accompanied by Barnabas and Mark (Acts 13:4). On later journeys it was Silvanus, Timothy, Titus, or others. The bond between them was not merely task-oriented; there was a deep bond of affection also. Paul likens his relationship with Timothy to that of a father and son (Phil 2:20–22). He calls Epaphroditus his "brother, co-worker, and comrade-in-arms" (Phil 2:25).

We find Paul's vision of a community in all his letters, especially in his First Letter to the Corinthians. His favorite image is that of the body: "For just as the body is one and has many members, and all the members of the body, though many, are one body, so it is with Christ" (12:12). The unifying element of this body is the Spirit of God, the source of all life: "For by one Spirit we were all baptized into one body—Jews or Greeks, slaves or free" (12:13). The image of the human body was chosen by Paul because it has the unique ability of having many specialized parts, and yet always functions as one.

Paul knows by insight what science has only recently discovered—
that the human body is really all in one and yet one in all. The original
one cell from which we developed had a complete image through its
genes and chromosomes of what the whole body would be. As billions
of other cells developed with all kinds of specialities, each new cell retained all the features of the original with one exception—that something
impeded it from developing a whole new body, which we call cloning.
Consequently, if one cell fails, another will take over its functions. If a
group of specialty cells fails, a neighboring group will gradually take on
its functions. There is no central cell or group of cells. The center is in
each and each is in the center.

Then Paul goes into the consequences of this unusual oneness in
diversity and diversity in oneness. These are: (1) A mutual dependence
and need of one another: "The eye cannot say to the hand, 'I have no
need for you,' nor again the head to the feet, 'I have no need of you' "
(12:20). In fact Paul shows that many of the weaker parts of the body
are actually the ones most needed of all. (2) The avoidance of disunity
and disharmony; in contrast the members should have a loving care for
one another: "that there may be no discord in the body, but that the members may have the same care for one another" (12:25). (3) Special mutual support in our difficulties and sufferings: "If one member suffers,
all suffer together."

We have seen, then, a beautiful picture of the interconnectedness
of each person within the Christian community. If one person has a gift
or special manifestation of the Spirit it is so that others can share in it.
All share in what comes to each, and each shares in what comes to all.
We might very well reason that this is fine if we are actually living together with others—but what if we are separated? Paul did not feel that
this mattered. He believed in what we now call the communion of
saints—that we can send to or receive effective help and loving support
from others. We find beautiful examples of this in Paul. He could even
be alone in prison and feel closer to others than most people feel with
many people around them. Here was his secret: whenever in quiet moments he thought of his friends, he prayed for them and sent them loving
energy and support. On the other hand, whenever he thought of God, he
prayed and remembered his friends as well. For example, on one occasion, Paul was alone and in prison in Greece. A death sentence might
come to him at any time. Yet he wrote to his close friends at Philippi a

letter which is the most joyful literature in the New Testament. He felt so close to his fellow Christians even though separated by hundreds of miles that he could write, "I thank God every time I think of you, praying for you with joy" (1:3). On the other hand, he trusts that their prayer and love will bring him special new joyous energy. He wrote, "Yes, and I shall rejoice. For I know that through your prayers and the help of the Spirit of Jesus Christ this will turn out for my deliverance" (1:19).

For Paul, however, the oneness within the community was not only spiritual and social, but economic as well. As a community of brothers and sisters, it was unthinkable that some might have more than enough food and material goods, while others would have little or nothing. That is why Paul was startled by news of the way that some Christians were celebrating Jesus' Last Supper. In those days, before celebrating the Lord's supper, the community had a common meal, where each family brought along the food they needed. Some of the richer households, however, prepared expensive banquets with plentiful liquor and gourmet foods. Other poor families had bread and little else. Paul wrote to the Corinthians that this was a terrible abuse contrary to the whole meaning of community and the Last Supper. He told them, "Do you despise the church of God, and humiliate those who have nothing?" (1 Cor 11:22). He then goes on to explain that the whole action of Jesus at the Last Supper was meant to be a model of sharing—even his own life—for others (1 Cor 11:25–35).

This ideal and practice of sharing was not merely a local matter, but part of a global concern that even broke down traditional barriers of race, culture and language. The Christian communities of Greece were economically much better off than communities in Israel, who were affected by a serious famine. Consequently in every community Paul established, he directed that a weekly collection be taken up and set aside to relieve hungry and poor people in Jerusalem. Community means equality, so Paul would write to the Corinthians:

> As a matter of equality, your abundance at the present time should supply their want, so that their abundance may supply your want, that there may be equality (2 Cor 8:14).

Some Notes for Practice: The mutual support found in a community is such an abundant source of energy and confidence that it would be a serious loss not to take full advantage of it. Larger church gatherings can provide some of this, yet it is important that this be supplemented by smaller meetings where members meet for meditation, sharing, prayer for one another's present needs, mutual action and even at times for celebration of the supper of the Lord. But like everything else, this takes initiative and work. We have to start it by actually inviting other people and showing that we want them. Meetings can take place in one's own home, or alternated in various homes. Each person or family can take turns in leading it. This means that no elaborate preparations are needed. All that is needed is a reading—usually from Scripture—a period of silence and reflection, then a time for sharing what the reading says to each person (notice this is not a discussion but a simple sharing of what each person feels in response to the reading). Then a period of prayer follows for the present needs of the members as they wish them expressed. Finally a concluding prayer or song together, or at times a sharing of bread and wine in memory of Jesus. Common or individual action can also be planned at this time to promote justice, human rights, etc.

The local community for Paul did not exist in isolation from the world around them. Just as each member or cell of the human body is a part of the whole and yet the whole is in each part, so it is with the whole world. Each person, then each local community, is a micro-cosm or little world. The world that we have often wanted to change is not *out there* but *we are the world*—part of it, and yet all of it in a mysterious way. As we change and grow, the whole world does so with us. The oneness, sharing and interconnectedness at the local level impels us to work for justice, order, and oneness in the whole world through effective action in cooperation with others.

Points for group or class discussion as well as individual reflection:

1. Describe the great secret of Paul the apostle that enabled him to be a "founder" of western Christianity. How can we make this our own and be energized from it?

2. What essential place did the Eucharist have in the secret of Paul? How can we relate the Eucharist to the realities of hunger and injustice in the world around us?

3. What are the distinguishing characteristics of a truly Christian community? In your experience, what has impeded you from finding a meaningful Christian community experience? What steps could you take to make it a great source of energy and support in your life?

Annotated Bibliography For Further Reading

Grassi, J., *The Secret of Paul the Apostle* (N.Y.: Orbis, 1978). Describes the inner motivation and ''secret of success'' of the man principally responsible for the spread of western Christianity.

Montague, G., *Building Christ's Body: The Dynamics of Christian Living According to St. Paul* (Chicago: Franciscan Herald, 1975). An explanation and practical application of Paul's dynamic personal insights to everyday Christian living.

13

Meditative Scripture Reading

1. Identification with the Text

It would be hard to overstate the importance of the Scriptures. God's story in the Bible and his story in the lives of each person must come together to produce fullness of life. It is difficult for the modern reader to understand that the Bible cannot simply be read as, say, the newspaper or modern literature. It was not written primarily to describe past events or people, but as a story to be *experienced and entered into.* This purpose is quite different from that of much modern writing which offers the reader merely an intellectual and academic exercise. For one thing, the Scriptures were not written for the silent reader to take in through his or her eyes. They were written to be publicly read aloud and *listened to.* In fact, the Hebrew Bible was *sung* aloud in ancient times so that listening could be a deeply felt experience.

The ancient Jewish way of "reading Scripture" was to identify as closely as possible with the story, entering into it as much as possible so that one participates in the whole drama. For example, in reading or hearing about the giving of the law on Mount Sinai, one should climb Mount Sinai with Moses, actually hear the thunder, see the lightning, and listen to the voice of God as addressed to oneself. Already in the Book of Deuteronomy we see this view of past events. The next generation after Moses is not to look back on these happenings in terms of the past, but to be actually at Mount Sinai with their forefathers. They themselves were there with Moses, hearing the thunder of God's voice:

> The Lord our God made a covenant with us in Horeb. Not with our fathers did the Lord make this covenant, but with us who are all of us here alive this day. The Lord spoke with you face to face at the mountain, out of the midst of the fire (5:2–4).

Another illustration of the ancient participatory way of reading Scripture is found in the way that past historical events were regarded; for example, the story of the exodus of the Jews from Egypt in Exodus 12—15. This was not looked upon as ancient history, a subject for academic study. It was considered as a present event in which all Jews past and present participate. For this reason, the passover ritual is very carefully described in the Book of Exodus. It is something that is to be constantly relived for countless thousands of years: "This day shall be for you a memorial day, and you shall keep it as a feast to the Lord; throughout your generations you shall observe it as an ordinance forever" (Ex 12:14). Even today, when the passover ritual is celebrated, it is regarded as a memorial feast. God's saving action is recalled precisely so that all the Jewish people may re-experience it as a present event. God is calling them here and now to liberation from slavery, whether to Egypt or any other nation, government, or institution. To bring out the present meaning, according to the biblical prescription, the children ask their father what is the meaning of the passover ritual: "And you shall tell your son on that day, 'It is because of what the Lord did for me when I came out of Egypt' " (Ex 13:8). The words "what the Lord did for *me*" are repeated each year in ritual and hold good for each person. For this reason, that particular verse is repeated several times for emphasis in the passover celebration.

A final example are the words Moses addressed to his people in Deuteronomy 6:4:

> Hear, O Israel! The Lord our God is one Lord; and you shall love the Lord, your God, with all your heart, and with all your soul, and with all your might.

God commanded that these words were to be repeated again and again, whether at home or on a journey, whether busy at work, or at rest. They were to be drilled into children, and written down on the very entrances of houses (6:7–9). These words of Scripture were taken so seriously by the Jews that this prayer was repeated many many times aloud during the day. The actual words were written in small parchments that were bound around their wrists and foreheads. Over the centuries who can say how many millions of times they have been prayed. The emphasis on God's oneness and total devotion sums up the essence of Judaism.

The New Testament writings were meant to be read in this same tradition. For example, each of the three Gospels describes how Jesus climbed a high mountain and was transfigured in glory before his disciples. The early Church understood this story not as something only *about* Jesus, but as a story they could enter into by being transfigured themselves through the grace of God. This is how the apostle Paul appears to understand it. He writes of this glory of God shining on the face of Jesus as follows: ''For it is God who said 'Let light shine out of darkness' who has shone in our hearts to give the light of the knowledge of the glory of God in the face of Christ'' (2 Cor 4:6). At the same time, he writes that this experience is shared by the Christian through union with Christ: ''And we all, with unveiled faces, beholding the glory of the Lord are being changed into his likeness from one degree of glory to another; for this comes from the Lord who is the Spirit'' (2 Cor 3:18).

Another way of understanding this participatory nature of Scripture is to regard it as a type of ''eternal drama.'' In other words, the people and events described are representative. They are telling us about what Jesus said and did not only to the twelve and his disciples but to you and me and ''everyman.'' As an example, we have in English the expression ''a doubting Thomas.'' This comes from the incident described by the Gospel of John (20:24–29). In this story, Thomas, one of the twelve, was not present when Jesus appeared to his disciples on the first Easter Sunday night. The other disciples told him that they had seen the Lord. Thomas replied, ''Unless I see in his hands the print of the nails, and place my finger in the mark of the nails, and place my hand in his side, I will not believe'' (20:25).

A week later the disciples were gathered together behind closed doors. This time Thomas was with them. Jesus appeared to them and said to Thomas: ''Put your finger here and see my hands; and put out your hand and place it in my side; do not be faithless but believing'' (20:27). As we have said, Thomas stands for us, the doubting Thomases of all times. We would like physical, tangible proof of everything. We want scientific, visual backing for all that we believe. Yet this is not accessible in faith. Without making the physical examination, Thomas makes a beautiful confession of faith in Jesus as God. No scientific explanation could have helped him to make this. He simply states, ''My

Lord and my God.'' The final statement of Jesus is addressed to all of us doubters like Thomas at any time: ''Have you believed because you have seen me? Blessed are those who have not seen and yet believe.'' (A question mark has been placed here in this RSV translation because the passage seems to mean that Thomas's vision and touch had nothing to do with believing Jesus was God.)

2. Second Basic Principle

Meditating on Scripture, when done in a ''sacred atmosphere,'' can be a source of special insights, as well as spiritual strength. By a ''sacred atmosphere'' we mean that Scripture must be read and meditated upon in the same spirit in which it was written. It was written *by* people of faith, *for* people of faith, and *in* a community of faith. St. Paul writes to Timothy, ''All Scripture is inspired by God and profitable for teaching, for reproof, for correction, and for training in righteousness that the man of God may be complete, equipped for every good work'' (2 Tim 3:16). The word ''inspired by God'' is one word in Greek: *theopneustos,* meaning literally ''blown into by God.'' The verse reflects a belief in the Church that Scripture first of all has its origin in a living community *inspired* by the Holy Spirit. The writer has a special gift of this Spirit in writing down what he and other members of the community believe. Finally he does this as a ministry of service for other believers as well.

Before reading or meditating on Scripture, it helps to try to recreate this sacred atmosphere. A short time of silence and preparatory prayer will be helpful, especially a prayer to the Spirit, the supreme author, for enlightenment. Once this sacred atmosphere is created, we can be ready for special messages that come to us through meditation on the Bible. It has always been believed that since God lies behind the biblical pages, there is a special message to listeners even beyond the immediate historical context of the particular passage.

Here are some examples of this outlook. In the Old Testament, Daniel one day reads in the prophet Jeremiah a prediction that in seventy years the people of Israel will return from exile (29:10). Daniel prays, fasts, and asks God what these words can mean for him and his people who are now in an entirely different time and historical context (Dn 9:1–27). A special answer about events hundreds of years later comes to him. He is told that the words in Jeremiah refer to seventy *weeks* of years, and speak of events pertaining to the Jewish people at the time the Book of Daniel was written.

Another example was the Qumran community, a group of pious Jews living a community religious life near the Dead Sea at the time of Jesus. They also had the same understanding of Scripture as referring to their own lives. They read in the Scriptures the prophet Isaiah's description of the return of the Jews from exile, using the words, "In the desert prepare the way of the Lord." They interpreted these words as especially referring to their own community many centuries later. In the words of Isaiah they felt they were preparing the way for the coming of the Messiah by their prayer, fasting, and religious life in the Judean desert.

In the New Testament, Mary the mother of Jesus appears to be reflecting on the meaning of the Scriptures just before an angel comes to her announcing that she will be the mother of the Messiah. The Scriptures seem to be those of Isaiah 7:14, "Therefore the Lord himself will give you a sign. Behold a virgin shall conceive and bear a son, and shall call his name Immanuel." The reason for suggesting that Mary is reflecting on Scripture is that the angel replies to her in the exact words of the Scripture (in the second person) as if giving her a new special meaning of the passage that applies to her life: "You shall conceive and bear a son and give him the name Jesus" (Lk 1:31). Another reason to support this is that biblical revelations usually come in response to a matter that a person is pondering over or reflecting about. Thus Joseph receives a dream from God telling him to go ahead with his espousal with Mary at the very time that he is concerned about what he should do in view of Mary's pregnancy (Mt 1:20).

The same approach to meditation on Sacred Scripture has continued through the centuries in Christian tradition. St. Augustine during the crisis that led to his conversion searched the Scriptures for guidance and strength. He found this in Romans 7, where Paul describes the struggle between the flesh and the spirit which is impossible to resolve by human strength alone. Augustine saw this duplicated in his own life as he struggled to be freed from a relationship that was chaining him to the flesh. In the passage in Romans he found that the grace of Christ could supply him the strength he needed so much. He applied to himself the words of Romans 7:25–26, "Who will deliver me from this body of death? Thanks be to God, through Jesus Christ our Lord." The same was true of Francis of Assisi. As a young man from a rich family he had been immersed in a self-centered life of luxury and pleasure. He heard from Scripture the words of Jesus, ''Go, sell what you have and give to the poor'' (Mk 10:21). He heard these words as God's voice personally addressed to him. As a result, he gave away all he had to the poor and hungry, devoting himself to a life of loving service of the sick, lepers, and the needy.

The final part of the ''sacred atmosphere'' of Scripture is found in the prayerful union with God, and the prayer that it inspires. Often this alone may be the meaning in our lives. Since Scripture is God speaking to us, when we listen to this voice, we naturally open ourselves to his love. We praise him and ask for all the strength we need in order to place his message into action in our daily life.

Exercises and examples: The story of the coming of the Holy Spirit on the early Church is found in chapters 1 and 2 of the Acts of the Apostles. In view of our understanding of Scripture, this is not a past event, but a continually repeated event in the Church. It repeats itself every time we duplicate the story in our own lives. (We might note that there are several other ''Pentecosts'' in the Acts of the Apostles—4:23–31; 10:44–48; 19:4–7. It is an event repeated again and again in the Church and in our own lives.)

First, begin with a prayer, a period of silence, and a reading of Acts 1—2. Then picture the event in your imagination so that you can be part of it. Imagine yourself on the scene with Peter and the apostles, Mary the mother of Jesus and the others. Wait and pray with them for the coming of the Holy Spirit. You can use the repeated short prayer ''Come, Holy Spirit'' along with them. Trust as they do that the Spirit will come, according to the promise of Jesus: ''I will send down upon you the promise of my Father'' (Lk 24:29). Feel and hear the sound like the rush of a mighty wind which was heard throughout the house where they were gathered (2:2). See in the center of the group the tongues of fire that appeared, parted and came to rest on each of them (2:3). Feel this flame, the love of the Holy Spirit descending on you, warming, strengthening and enlightening your whole being. Perceive how this same flame unites you to everyone else as well. You share their power and love as they share yours. Send some of this energy to someone who especially needs it. Direct the energy also to some area of your life that needs special direction and attention. Feel your entire being "filled with the Holy Spirit" (2:4). Study how you can bring this Spirit to others, proclaiming it by your life and actions (2:4).

Another example might be the story of the transfiguration of Jesus (Mk 9:1–8; Mt 17:1–3; Lk 9:28–36). First read the passage. Then imagine Jesus asking you to climb the mountain along with Peter, James, and John in order to be together with him in a very special manner. Picture yourself making the difficult climb of the high mountain. While weary of body, you are happy to be chosen for this privilege and you follow the footsteps of your Guide. When you reach the top of the mountain, you notice Jesus off by himself in prayer. Inspired by his example, you begin to pray also. As Jesus prays, you see the sun envelop his whole being so that his face shines like the sun, and his clothes become a dazzling white. You ask God to be close to Jesus and share his glory. Suddenly you feel the warm rays of the sun permeate your whole being. Your own face becomes luminous as the rays of God's glory come to you from Jesus. You let your whole being in its depths feel this light, warmth and strength. You notice that your companions too are all part of this shining glory of Jesus. With them you say to Jesus, "How good it is for us to be here" (Mk 9:5). Then you see a bright cloud overshadow all of you and a thunderous voice from heaven proclaim, "This is my Son, my beloved. Listen to him" (9:7). You feel these words addressed not only to Jesus, but to yourself also. You experience new inner power as you realize that you too are a Son of God because of your union with Jesus. Then, when the experience on the mountain is ended, you descend full of joy and strength with Jesus. Jesus comes down the mountain and heals a desperately sick young man (9:14–29). You likewise bring wholeness and healing into the people and situations that you will face in life. Imagine them even before they take place.

A final example is a very effective way of combining a powerful transforming mantra (see Chapter 3) with meditation on Scripture. Reflect on the short scene in John 20:19–23 where the risen Jesus appears to his disciples on Easter Sunday night and breathes upon them the gift of the Holy Spirit. Imagine yourself within that group, fearful, behind closed doors, waiting and praying for Jesus to come with the promised gift of the Holy Spirit. Suddenly he comes in the midst of your group, despite the fact that the doors have been locked. He greets you and the others with the words, ''Peace be with you.'' As he does, you feel the gift of peace enter the center of your being. With the others, you rejoice at the sight and presence of the risen Lord. He then says to you, ''As the Father has sent me, so I send you.'' You gratefully receive from Jesus the mission to go out into the world in love and service to duplicate his work. You feel confident you can do it because it is a direct commission from him. Then Jesus breathes upon you and says, ''Receive the Holy Spirit. If you forgive the sins of any, they are forgiven.'' Keeping the image of the risen Jesus before you, you breathe in the gift of the Spirit as he breathes it out to you. Keep repeating this until you feel your whole being refreshed with the presence of the Spirit. Since Jesus has said that the Spirit embodies love and forgiveness, you send this forgiveness and love to those who especially need it. This may be someone you have hurt, or someone who has hurt you. Combine now the early Christian mantra, ''Come, Holy Spirit,'' with the Scripture scene. As you breathe in and Jesus breathes out the Holy Spirit, say to yourself, ''Come, Holy Spirit,'' with each in-breath. As you breathe out, in order to emphasize the gift of love and forgiveness, you can repeat, ''Fill our hearts with love.'' This combination of both Scripture meditation and prayer mantra can be a most moving experience as well as a quick way to move toward spiritual growth and renewal.

By way of summary, the secret of meditation of Scripture is (1) participation and involvement, finding ourselves as part of the eternal drama of the biblical stories, as we see them repeated again and again in our lives; (2) recovering the ''sacred atmosphere'' of Scripture. The inspired word of God is his instrument to speak to us here and now about what is meaningful in our lives. The word of God is meant to bring us into intimate contact with his very being itself. It is also meant to be the special medium by which the word and example of Jesus as well as the presence of the Holy Spirit can be part of our daily lives.

Annotated Bibliography for Further Reading

J. Grassi, *The Spiritual Message of the Gospels* (Canfield, Ohio: Alba Communications, 1979). A cassette recorded series composed of reflections on the Gospel passages as related to personal growth in a modern world setting.

Gill, John, *Images of My Self* (Ramsey, N.Y.: Paulist, 1982). A handbook for meditation and self-exploration through the imagery of the Gospels.

McDonnell, R., *Prayer Pilgrimage Through Scripture* (Ramsey, N.J.: Paulist, 1984). A valuable guide to using the senses, memory, imagination and emotions on a prayerful journey through the Scriptures.

14

The Daily Journal as a Means of Personal Growth

To conclude our book we would like to make some suggestions about the use of a daily journal. This is a very effective means of applying the personal and spiritual growth process to the events of each day.

A journal entry is usually written during a quiet time in the evening when we have fewer distractions and can look back meditatively over the day. A special notebook should be set aside for the daily journal. A looseleaf type to which filler pages can be added or taken off is especially handy.

The daily journal is not just a diary of impressions of each day, although it may well include these. It need not be very long, but there are a number of matters that should always be included. It should start with the month, day and date so that back reference can be made each day to a week ago, a month, six months and a year or further. This will help us detect longer trends in our life or cycles of meaning. Often the meaning of a dream or an event may not come for weeks or months.

The following areas can be noted:

1. Dreams of last night—a short description and notes on their meaning as explained in Chapter 4.
2. The significant events and encounters of the day: how they influenced us and how we have reacted to them. What meaning do they have for us in view of our life goals? What is the most important thing I have learned today?
3. Under S.E. (separating emotions) we should note the situation and the causes or addiction behind them (cf. Chapter 7). If we have not already healed or reprogrammed them, we should immediately stop to do so according to the instructions in that chapter. For positive re-

115

inforcement, we can also note under U.E. (unifying emotions) when we have experienced peace, oneness and total attention through dedicated living and listening.

4. In the journey of personal growth, there are many paths. We cannot effectively use all these at once. It is helpful to concentrate on a "Practice of the Week" and note how well we have done. For example, we may choose one week to make more effective use of our Inner Guide as in Chapter 4. Another week we may give more special attention to awareness of separating emotions and their remedy as in Chapter 6.

5. A final but most important part of the daily journal should be given to progress in development of the will. Without strengthening of the will, we will never make effective progress. This is better done by a special part of the journal book rather than under each date. In Chapters 5 and 6 about the will, we had the "I can't, I won't, I will" exercise in which, during the last step, we noted something definite we would shortly do in order to make possible the fulfillment of our intentions. In this special notebook section, we can have one looseleaf page entitled "Tomorrow," another, "During the Week," another "During the Month," and possibly another under "Six Months." The entries should be made in the feeling that we simply cannot count on many years ahead. Death can come at any time (cf. Chapter 9), and we should live with tentatively only six months left. Under each entry page we should note what we plan to do tomorrow (or next week, etc.) that will promote our personal growth or something that will be a matter of loving service to others. Each day we should carefully note our progress in fulfilling these plans so our will becomes strengthened as a more effective instrument for personal growth. We can also note other smaller things we want to do as ways of acting decisively each day.

After our journal work, it is a good practice to devote some time to "spiritual reading." The best such reading is the Bible or books written by authors who have lived according to the highest ideals. At the end of the reading or journal work, it would be a fitting conclusion to pray alone or with others. Some of the Psalms of David are particularly helpful. They have a universal poetic and spiritual tone that can nourish and strengthen our deepest aspirations.

Finally, and this is the last point of our book: we should always keep in mind the urgent importance of image-making in our work of transforming the universe. Through our persistent images, we actually make the world what we really want it to be. The daily journal can play a very important role in this. As we noted above, we can strengthen our wills by definite decisions for tomorrow, one week, etc. To this we can unite the dynamic power of image making. To illustrate, this book has been in my "six months to a year" column in my journal. I thought of it each day, imagining each step in the process: completing each chapter, sending it to the publisher, seeing the finished bound copy. I saw you the reader going through it. In other words, the *secret is to imagine the future as already happening*. This focuses all the energies needed to bring a project to completion. We can apply this to every effort we make to develop a meaningful whole earth spirituality that can play a vital part in making our world what it is meant to be—a world of love, oneness, justice and peace.

Annotated Bibliography For Further Reading

Progroff, Ira, *At A Journal Workshop* (N.Y.: Dialogue House Workshop, 1975). The author and his staff have given very effective Journal workshops throughout the U.S.

Simons, G.F., *Keeping Your Personal Journal* (Ramsey, N.J.: Paulist, 1978). A very practical book with detailed suggestions on how to use journals as vehicles for personal growth.